CHRISTIANS
in the
AMERICAN REVOLUTION

CHRISTIANS
in the
AMERICAN REVOLUTION

by Mark A. Noll

A Subsidiary of Christian College Consortium
and Wm. B. Eerdmans Publishing Company

Library of Congress Cataloging in Publication Data
Noll, Mark A.   1946-
    Christians in the American Revolution.
    Bibliography: p. 177
    1. United States—History—Revolution,   1775-1783—Religious
aspects.   2. United States—Church history—Colonial period, ca. 1600-
1775.   I. Title.
E209.N64   277.3   77-23354
ISBN 0-8028-1706-8

Grateful acknowledgment is made for permission to quote from the
following sources:

Material from Walter Herbert Stowe, "Some Aspects of the Relations
of the Clergy to the State," *Historical Magazine of the Protestant Episcopal Church,* XIX (December 1950). Used with permission of the
Church Historical Society.

Material from the *Mennonite Historical Bulletin,* XXXV (July 1974).
Used with permission of the Historical Committee of the Mennonite
Church.

Material from *The Price of Loyalty: Tory Writings from the Revolu-
tionary Era,* edited by Catherine S. Crary (copyright © 1973 by
McGraw-Hill Book Company). Used with permission of McGraw-Hill
Book Company.

Material from Dorothy Gilbert Thorne, "North Carolina Friends and
the Revolution," *The North Carolina Historical Review,* XXXVIII
(July 1961). Used with permission of the North Carolina Division of
Archives and History.

Excerpts from Peter Brock, *Pacifism in the United States: From the
Colonial Era to the First World War* (copyright © 1961 by Princeton
University Press), pp. 3-306. Reprinted by permission of Princeton
University Press.

An abridged rendering of chapter five appeared as "Tory Believers:
Which Higher Loyalty?" in *Christianity Today,* July 2, 1976, pp. 6-9.
The material published in that essay is used here by permission.

To Francis A. and Evelyn J. Noll
Parents, Patrons, Fellow-Heirs

Acknowledgments

My friend, Nathan Orr Hatch, offered a great deal of indirect personal encouragement during the writing of this book. His scholarly work on Christianity and the American Revolution provided a more direct sort of aid, as for example the definition of ideology in the preface and the general picture in Chapter Three of how patriotic and Christian ideas intermingled. Those who desire more serious study of the matters sketched here could do far worse than look into Professor Hatch's own new book, *The Sacred Cause of Liberty: Republican Thought and the Millennium in Revolutionary New England.* His assistance notwithstanding, the errors in the book are all mine.

My wife Maggie and my daughter Mary kept me anchored in the real world of the twentieth century while I was trying to discover real worlds in the eighteenth. Without them, this project, not to speak of life itself, would be much impoverished. Jim Ohlson, Dick and Jo Peters, Robert and Ruth Packer, and Milt Hale helped along the way more than they knew. Professors Richard C. Wolf and Douglas E. Leach of Vanderbilt University had nothing to do with this book directly, but their diligent criticism of another project forced me to think clearly about some of the ideas presented here. My greatest debt is discharged, however inadequately, by the dedication.

Contents

Preface

The General Association of Congregational ministers in Connecticut, meeting in June of 1761, had little pressing theological or ecclesiastical business. Some of the ministers were indeed still concerned about issues thrust up by the great revival of the 1740's, but the disruption which had marked the revival had now been replaced by a greater tolerance for theological differences and an increased interest in other matters. If the General Association had scant ecclesiastical business on its agenda, other matters did call for attention: the war with infidel France had begun to turn in favor of the British Empire, and a new king, George III, had succeeded to the English throne since the Association had last met.

The meeting took note of these events in an official letter to the new sovereign.

> We thankfully Adore the good Providence of God, which has crowned [the War with France] with signal Success in every part of the World, and especially in America where the Designs of your Majesty's Enemies have been utterly defeated. . . . And as the Churches under our Care have always distinguished themselves by their Loyalty and Obedience, we humbly recommend them and Our Selves to your Majesty's favor and Protection, and we shall make it our constant Care to inculcate upon them Submission to your Majesty's Government and Authority, which we shall endeavour to enforce by our own example.[1]

1. *The Records of the General Association of Ye Colony of Connecticut,* ed. Lavallette Perrin (Hartford: Case, Lockwood & Brainard, 1888), pp. 46-47.

Fifteen years later the same body, meeting again in June, wrote another letter, this one "to the CONSOCIATED PASTORS and CHURCHES" of Connecticut. Instead of entreating the people to praise God for his blessings, it called for repentance in order to remove a scourge from the land; instead of assuring the king of faithful loyalty, it raised grave questions about the relationship between Britain and her colonies. Connecticut, in the Association's words, had been

> reduced by the arbitrary edicts of the British Parliament, and the cruel and inhuman Methods used to inforce them to the sad Necessity of defending by Force and Arms those precious Privileges which our Fathers fled into this Wilderness quietly to enjoy: [they had been] Declared Rebels by the British King and Parliament.

The General Association further charged that

> a large Army of Foreign Mercenaries, hired at a most extravagant Price, [has been] employed to dragoon us into Obedience, or rather abject Submission to Tyranny. . . . Our Children, our Friends, our dearest Connections [have been] called from our Bosoms to the Field of Battle; and some of them captivated and enslaved by our cruel and insulting Foes: Detestible Parricides [are] interspersed among us, aiming to give a fatal stab to the Country which gave them birth, and hath hitherto fostered them in her indulgent Bosom.[2]

In the fifteen years which intervened between the General Association's pledge of fealty to George III and its indictment of British actions against the American colonies, momentous events and decisions had unhinged the political bond linking Great Britain and her principal North American possessions. Equally momentous arguments had been produced by the colonists to justify this political division. These arguments were derived originally from English sources but had been nourished and brought to fruition in America. They placed supreme value in personal and corporate freedom

---

2. *Ibid.,* p. 89.

and were extremely sensitive to the corruptions of government which threatened to undermine liberty. The presence of these ideas even in the General Association's pastoral letter testifies to their pervasive grip on the colonial mind.

Among Christians in the colonies, however, it was not only the Congregationalists of Connecticut who were involved in the events and who shared the ideas and attitudes which led to the War for Independence. Colonial Christians of every stripe participated in and influenced the movement toward independence. In turn, the course of the Revolution deeply affected colonial church bodies and their grasp of Christian truth. Individual Christians took varied courses of action in response to the Revolutionary crisis, and widely dissimilar motives often lay behind the outwardly similar reactions to the Revolution's events and ideas. Yet almost without exception, Christians in the colonies were unable, even if they had been willing, to avoid the public debate and the private decisions which led to a new nation in the new world.

As used in this study, the "American Revolution" refers more to "the Revolution . . . in the minds and hearts of the people" of which John Adams would later write[3] than to the political and military events before and during the War for Independence itself. These political and military events are important and will not be slighted here, but it will also be necessary to remember that economic, social, and cultural factors played significant roles in the course of the Revolution. The primary concern of this book, however, is the way in which religious convictions and Revolutionary thought interacted in the minds and hearts of American Christians. Or put in another way, the book is a comparative study of religious and Revolutionary ideology in eighteenth-century America where ideology is considered

---

3. An excellent general discussion and critique of the different ways in which the "American Revolution" has been understood throughout American history is provided by Edmund S. Morgan in his article, "The American Revolution: Revisions in Need of Revising," and his editorial introductions to the other articles in *The American Revolution: Two Centuries of Interpretation,* ed. Edmund S. Morgan (Englewood Cliffs, N.J.: Prentice-Hall, 1965).

to be those historical reconstructions and projections, moral judgments, and images of self and of foes through which human groups express their highest aspirations, reveal their deepest values, define their desired place in history, and rally themselves in the face of crises.

Chapters Three through Six of this study review the varied paths colonial Christians took in response to the Revolution. Some supported the move for independence and the concept of a free United States without reservation. Some exploited the ideas justifying the break with Great Britain in order to argue for changes in American society. Other Christians refused to support the drive for independence because of their deep-seated convictions against political and military conflict. And still others remained loyal to the mother country. These chapters do not pretend to offer an exhaustive account of the ways in which Christians reacted to the Revolution. Their purpose is, rather, to explain the internal nature and external consequences of four widespread and contrasting Christian responses to the crisis.

In order to see these responses in context, Chapter One provides a brief sketch of British-American relations in the eighteenth century, and Chapter Two traces the course of American religious history over the same period. Without this background one cannot properly understand the ways in which Christians in the colonies helped to shape the course of the Revolution or how American Christianity was influenced by the struggle for independence.

This struggle for independence has naturally received much attention through recent bicentennial observances. This attention to national history poses a challenge for contemporary Christians in America to reassess their relationship with the nation, its stated policies, and its political processes. Christians, like all other Americans, are affected by national political decisions and are privileged to help define and implement national values. Recent concern for public ethics and for the moral implications of national policy in such diverse areas as defense, agriculture, and the environment provides Christians an opportunity to contribute to the national discussion of values, priorities, and purposes. To do this knowledgeably, they must not ignore the religious history of the United States, particularly its origin, for the religious-national connection forged at the time of the American Revolution has exerted a dominant influence in the history of the United States to the present day. This connection and its impact on American history will be examined in the last chapter.

This book does not pretend to be the definitive scholarly treatment of its topic. It represents, rather, an attempt to trace with broad strokes the story of Christian participation in the public life of the Revolutionary period. I have said too little to satisfy experts in the field, and probably too much to entirely please those with no previous experience in the study of early American history. Yet for scholars, novices, and those in between, the book offers what we have lacked for too long: a sympathetic, yet critical, historical overview of Christians in the American Revolution.

I   *Prelude to War*

"The shot heard 'round the world" was fired at Lexington Green on April 19, 1775. Immediately thereafter, British and colonial spokesmen presented strikingly different accounts of what had taken place. On April 22, Lieutenant Colonel Smith of the British 10th Foot wrote matter-of-factly to Governor Gage: "In obedience to your Excellency's commands, I marched on the evening of the 18th inst. with the corps of grenadiers and light infantry for Concord, to execute your Excellency's orders with respect to destroying all ammunition, artillery, tents, etc., collected there, which was effected."[1] The Provincial Congress of Massachusetts, meeting at Watertown, issued its official response to the military action on April 26. This report castigated the British soldiers for wanton destruction of life and property and called public attention to callous atrocities said to have been committed by the redcoats. Unlike Lieutenant Colonel Smith, the colonials were quick to see the events as part of a larger, more meaningful whole: "These ... are marks of ministerial vengeance against this colony, for refusing, with her sister colonies, a submission to slavery. ... To the persecution and tyranny of [the king's] cruel ministry we will not tamely submit — appealing to Heaven for the justice of our cause, we determine to die or be free."[2]

---

1. *Documents of American History*, Vol. I: *To 1898*, ed. Henry Steele Commager, 8th ed. (New York: Appleton-Century-Crofts, 1968), 90.
2. *Ibid.*, p. 89.

The skirmish at Lexington and Concord was but the last in a long series of events about which British and colonial spokesmen had been unable to agree on an interpretation. The colonists wondered how Parliament and the king's ministry could be so vile as to expect them to sit idly while tyrannical assaults threatened their rights of property and self-defense. Parliament, for its part, could not understand how the colonials expected to command the respect of judicious men if the simple steps necessary to maintain public peace in the colonies were painted in the livid colors of moral outrage.

This inability to agree on the significance of British actions and the character of colonial responses was nearly total. Since the close of the French and Indian War (known as the Seven Years' War in England), event after event had stimulated the most impassioned controversy. To what were, in British eyes, simple and uncomplicated moves to consolidate the great gains of the Seven Years' War and to put in order the economic affairs of a vastly expanded empire, the colonists persisted in taking determined and vociferous offense.

The intensity of the disagreement was all the more remarkable in light of the unity of purpose displayed during the war with France. The colonists and the British alike had rejoiced in the great victories of that *annus mirabilis,* 1759: the daring triumph of General Wolf over the Marquis de Montcalm at Quebec which issued in the British acquisition of Canada, the smashing defeats of the French navy that left Britannia undisputed mistress of the seas, and the convincing successes in India which opened that vast subcontinent to control and exploitation by the British empire. The accession of George III in 1760 and the successful culmination of the war were hailed from Maine to Georgia. In addition, colonists who had suffered long and impatiently from the assaults of French and Indians on the frontier welcomed the Treaty of Paris of 1763 that formalized the ouster of France from its mainland possessions in the New World.

No sooner, however, had the British ministry moved

to organize its conquests and regularize their administration than protests began in the American colonies. It is probably true that various developments in the colonies, well established before 1763, would have led to discord or estrangement from Great Britain apart from the new imperial tension following the French and Indian War. These included the tradition of independent legislatures and the tendency to headstrong political behavior, the greater social flexibility and somewhat greater receptivity to participatory democracy, the rapidly growing population and the embarrassment of natural resources, and the tensions inherent in a mercantile system when an exploited feeder region begins to think in terms of its own industrial and commercial development. Yet it is no exaggeration to say that British efforts after 1763 to organize and consolidate the empire led quite directly, and over a very short period of time, to the loss of that empire's most profitable possessions.

This sudden trouble in the new and gloriously expanded empire was a perplexity from the British point of view. Parliament certainly did not intend that the steps taken after the Treaty of Paris in 1763 should lead to the Treaty of Paris in 1783 which officially recognized the independence of the American colonies. Furthermore, those events between 1763 and the opening of hostilities which so greatly aroused patriotic colonials seemed innocuous to British eyes.

The Proclamation of 1763 which created royal districts in North America between the Mississippi and the Appalachians proposed merely to regularize the administration of a region in which rival colonial and English land claims and the threats of still hostile Indians created much uncertainty. The Sugar Act of 1764 was nothing but a revision and restructuring of the Molasses Act of 1733. It was designed to insure that the central principle underlying the British Navigation Acts of the seventeenth century would be preserved: that the exports from the British colonies would work for the economic well-being of Great Britain and not for Britain's European rivals or their possessions in the West Indies. If the various Navigation Acts of the seventeenth and early eighteenth centuries had been enforced laxly, par-

ly under the Walpole and Newcastle administrations,
ercantile principles of the Acts had been patently clear
from the outset and had never elicited more than casual
colonial grumbling.

That great colonial bugaboo, the Stamp Act, was
to George Grenville, prime minister from 1763 to 1765,
nothing but a modest plan for the colonists to share in the
expenses of defending the western frontier against the Indians
and to do their fair share in easing the crush of Britain's
war debt. After all, it had been no small thing for Great
Britain to remove the French from the frontier and to make
the seas safe for American ships. Charles W. Akers, a recent
biographer of Jonathan Mayhew, one colonial clergyman
who took decided exception to the British interpretation of
the Stamp Act, sets out the British case with clarity:

> In English eyes the revenue question was
> simple. The British debt was staggering; the American
> debt insignificant. Englishmen paid high taxes; Ameri-
> cans low taxes. Much of the British debt had been
> acquired defending the colonies from the French, and
> now the territory to guard and administer had been en-
> larged by the recent war. Therefore, tax revenues from
> the colonies must be increased.[3]

Considered in terms of the needs of the empire, the Stamp
Act with its projected annual revenue of £100,000 was but
a small price for the colonists to pay in easing an English
debt that had grown some £130,000,000 during the recent
war.

A similar construction was placed on other official measures of the 1760's and 1770's which struck so many
colonials as "tyrannical." When it became clear that a colonial agreement not to import goods from England and
resistance within the colonies to the special tax rendered
the Stamp Act ineffective, Parliament repealed it but at
the same time passed the Declaratory Act of March, 1766.
This piece of legislation reminded the colonists that the gov-

---

3. Charles W. Akers, *Called unto Liberty: A Life of Jonathan Mayhew, 1720-1766* (Cambridge: Harvard University Press, 1964), p. 198.

ernment in London, and not the individual provincial legislatures, was the source of final governmental authority in
the empire and declared that the king sitting in Parliament
had "full power and authority to make laws and statutes
of sufficient force and validity to bind the colonies and people of *America,* subjects of the crown of *Great Britain,* in
all cases whatsoever."[4] As much as this declaration affronted
colonial presumption, it merely expressed explicitly what the
mercantile system had always implied. The Townshend duties
of 1767 did not alter the fundamental character of earlier
Navigation Acts and further aided imperial efficiency by
applying some of the new revenues to the salaries of governors and justices in the royal colonies. The infamous Tea
Act of 1773 sought to balance supply and demand within
the empire. By allowing tea from the East India Company
to pass to colonial markets without the payment of duties,
it aided that struggling venture while at the same time making great quantities of tea available to the colonists at prices
well below those they had been forced to pay in the past.
How the bitter complaints of a few New England merchants
who seemed incapable of placing the general benefits of cheap
tea above their own private interests could stir up so many
people was an unfathomable mystery to the British ministry.

Stir them up it did, however, and on that famous
December night in 1773, three shiploads of English tea were
dumped into Boston harbor. The series of measures enacted
to restore order in the Boston area, called by the colonists
the "Intolerable Acts," did indeed close the harbor, provide
for the quartering of British troops, transfer customs cases
to other jurisdictions, and take the authority of naming the
Massachusetts Council out of the hands of the colonists.
But these were not extraordinary deprivations for a city that
had anarchistically destroyed great amounts of government-
backed property and for a provincial government which refused to move against the lawbreakers.

The colonial uproar over the Quebec Act of 1774
was, from a British perspectve, similarly inexplicable. Here

---

4. *Documents of American History,* Vol. I, 61.

was a measure granting the very religious freedom to the inhabitants of Quebec which the more southern colonies had often claimed as the cause of original settlements in the New World. Roman Catholics in Quebec were granted the right to practice their religion so long as they maintained political allegiance to Great Britain, just as Congregationalists in New England and Presbyterians in New Jersey were so privileged. What reasonable being could fathom the cries of outrage at the passage of this act? And then came the gunfire on the 19th of April, 1775. No sensible person with the best interests of the empire at heart could take offense at the march to Concord, for it was quite evidently suicidal for any government to allow its citizens to arm themselves promiscuously beyond control of the law.

These British actions were of course capable of a radically different interpretation from a colonial perspective, and this perspective has been the dominant one in the writing of American history. From the colonial point of view, the practical steps to organize the British empire assumed sinister overtones and loomed as threats to the individual and corporate liberties which had only been gained after long and arduous struggle throughout the history of the English people.

The colonial Patriots and their British sympathizers could not agree with imperial spokesmen on the wisdom of a single one of the pragmatic moves taken to consolidate the empire. The Proclamation of 1763 appeared to strike at the colonial charters in which land rights were often granted from the Atlantic to the Pacific; it also frustrated the efforts of colonial land speculators to gain a stake in the trans-Appalachian region. The Sugar Act of 1764 and the entire effort to tighten the English mercantile system appeared to jeopardize the basic human right of benefiting from the labor of one's own hands since it deprived colonial merchants of income to which lengthy usage had made them accustomed. By shutting them off from the French Indies, it further robbed the colonists of the major source of hard money with which they had paid debts owed to English merchants. The violent storm which greeted the

Stamp Act in the colonies reflected the conviction that the Act deprived the colonists of their property without due process of law. If the Americans could be taxed without their own consent or the consent of their duly elected representatives, what guarantee existed that a similar exercise of arbitrary power would not strip them of all their worldly goods and even threaten their persons? Parliament's declaration that it could bind the colonies "in all cases whatsoever" only heightened this apprehension. The provision of the Townshend duties which applied custom revenues to the salaries of colonial governors and justices also frightened Americans. With the power of the purse removed, the last check on royal government in the colonies was transferred from a general citizenry of native virtue to a ministry which many Americans saw as defiled by venality and hamstrung by corruption. The Tea Act galled Americans not because it provided cheap beverages, but because, once again, Parliament had threatened colonial prosperity by an arbitrary act. To grant the East India Company a monopoly on tea in the colonies without securing the assent of the colonial merchants merely added to British violations of property rights. Resistance to the Tea Act, as earlier to the Stamp Act, was not subversive but in fact a defense of the principles of the English "constitution" and of the hard-won liberties of Englishmen everywhere. The Intolerable Acts showed where the inclination to unlimited political power led: the Quartering Act violated the right to one's own home, the Port Bill abrogated the right to enjoy the fruits of one's own toil, the right to trial by one's peers was casually dismissed by the Administration of Justice Act, and the right to select one's own legislature was usurped by the Massachusetts Government Act. If the Intolerable Acts were not proof enough of Great Britain's designs on colonial liberties, the Quebec Act was. To establish Roman Catholicism — infamous propagator of the Inquisition and self-confessed foe of freedom in religion and government — as the official religion of a neighboring jurisdiction confirmed the worst fears that the religious liberty so precious to the American colonists resided under a dark cloud. Was not the imposition of Roman tyranny in Quebec but a prelude to the imposition of Anglican bishops in the colonies and the consequent cessation of first religious and then all liberties? Finally, the assault on lightly armed yeomen at Lexington and Concord was the last manifestation of the unprincipled lust for power so consistently present in British policies after the French and Indian War. The wanton destruction of human life which the 19th and 20th of April witnessed was a harbinger of things to come for all colonists if the British behemoth were left to its own devices.

The antithetical constructions placed by colonists and Parliament on British actions from 1763 to 1775 were manifestations of a deeper antithesis between pragmatic concerns in the English ministry and ideological concerns in the colonies. The nature of politics in eighteenth-century England was such that lofty principles of English liberty did not exert appreciable influence in the running of the empire. Two extrinsic factors were, by themselves, almost enough to assure this insensitivity. The strain of assimilating the vast chunks of new land secured from France demanded immediate administrative decisions and did not allow leisure for detached and solicitous consideration of freedom and right. The instability of British government during this period, with seven prime ministers in George III's first decade as king, prevented Great Britain, even if it had wanted to, from constructing a balanced policy toward the American colonies which was able to take into consideration both British imperial needs and American concerns for liberty.

Considerable doubt exists, however, that significant numbers of English politicians in the period were concerned with balanced policy, abstract concepts of liberty, or anything other than self-aggrandizement and jockeying for advantage in Parliament. The Whig "party" which dominated eighteenth-century English politics until Lord North's appointment as Prime Minister in 1770 was a maze of tangled interest groups and factions which, with occasional exceptions like William Pitt or Edmund Burke, shunned ideological principles as guidelines for actions and wandered in the directionless muddle that besets pragmatism in its purer forms.

The absence of a significant democratic check on many of the members of Parliament, elected from tightly controlled electorates or from the infamous "rotten boroughs," left effective control of Parliamentary action in the hands of a limited number of wealthy and well-placed Whig families. Even George III, in attempting to reassert the king's constitutional role as chief executive, was led by the political exigencies of the time into the warrens of influence peddling and patronage. Incompetence in government could be tolerated if only it was loyal.

It was not as if the principles of natural and individual rights which had broken into the open during the Puritan Revolution of the seventeenth century and which, refined and restrained, had been made a part of the British constitution at the time of the Glorious Revolution (1688) had vanished from England. Much to the contrary. The conviction that the disposition of power was at the heart of the political process, that unchecked power led to corruption and corruption to unchecked power, and that the arbitrary exercise of unchecked power must by its very nature result in the demise of liberty, law, and natural rights continued to be proclaimed in the eighteenth century. Early in the century John Trenchard and Thomas Gordan gave effective expression to these beliefs in a weekly paper, the *Independent Whig*. Later in the century the works of the radical libertarians of the Puritan Revolution were reissued by individuals who sought to inculcate the principles of personal freedom, restrained government, and wariness of official corruption. Closer to the time of the American Revolution, Thomas Hollis, whom Bernard Bailyn has called "that extraordinary one-man propaganda machine in the cause of liberty,"[5] and James Burgh, whose *Political Disquisitions* systematically expounded the thought of these "Real" Whigs, emerged as prominent spokesmen for ideological libertarianism in England. But in contrast to the period of the Glorious Revolution, when such ideas had been championed by the leaders of English government, these later libertarians

---

5. Bernard Bailyn, *The Ideological Origins of the American Revolution* (Cambridge: Harvard University Press, 1967), p. 40.

were forced to develop their ideas outside of Parliament. The limited group of wealthy Whig landowners in whose hands Parliamentary power was concentrated included no ardent libertarians. Having been frustrated in their efforts to break into this inner circle and to transform their ideas into official policy, the Real Whigs turned to literary effort. Their message, though presented with vigor and cogency, fell on deaf ears at a time when the day-to-day concerns of manning the empire and maneuvering for political position dominated the attention of the ruling Whig groups.

If libertarian ideas carried little weight in England during the eighteenth century, they made up for it in the American colonies. As has been noted, colonial perceptions of British actions after the French and Indian War were in the abstract terms of power, rights, and freedom. A deep-seated fear of conspiratorial action against liberty gripped many individuals. The tangled state of English politics and the apparent concessions to venality confirmed this fear. Given this frame of mind, how else could the Stamp Act, the stringent Navigation Acts, the Quebec Act, and the Intolerable Acts be seen except as assaults on liberty arising from the corrupt and arbitrary exercise of unchecked power?

The Virginia Resolves at the time of the Stamp Act had outlined a basic colonial position. Since it was only by one's duly elected representatives that taxes could be levied, "every attempt to vest such power in any person or persons whatsoever other than the General Assembly aforesaid has a manifest tendency to destroy British as well as American freedom."[6] By 1775 the convictions about human right and freedom which the Stamp Act had begun to precipitate were receiving their final form. On July 6 of that year, the Continental Congress issued a proclamation justifying the use of arms against Great Britain. It began by denying that it was proper for "a part of the human race to hold an absolute property in, and an unbounded power over others . . . ," and it explained the actions of Parliament toward the colonies as the manifestations of an unsatiable lust for unbridled power:

---

6. *Documents of American History,* Vol. I, 56.

> The legislature of Great-Britain, ... stimu-
> lated by an inordinate passion for a power not only un-
> justifiable, but which they know to be peculiarly repro-
> bated by the very constitution of that kingdom, and
> desperate of success in any mode of contest, where re-
> gard should be had to truth, law, or right, have at
> length, deserting those, attempted to effect their cruel
> and implicit purpose of enslaving these colonies by
> violence, and have thereby rendered it necessary for
> us to close with their last appeal from reason to arms.[7]

In sum, British actions threatened the fundamental liberties
without which meaningful human existence stood in jeopardy.
To resist these threats was not rebellion but an evidence of
true virtue.

The arguments against Great Britain did not, however, remain merely on the level of power, personal corruption, and natural liberty. Transcendent values were also
brought into the picture. Throughout the rhetoric of colonial dissent ran a deep vein of religiously charged discourse
which the colonists mined persistently and vigorously. They
called God to witness the injustices under which the colonies
labored and claimed divine origin for the rights threatened
by Great Britain. Patrick Henry's famous speech of March
23, 1775, which ended in the cry for liberty or death, abound-
ed in references to the colonies' privileges and responsibilities
under God. He urged the colonials to "make a proper use
of those means which the God of nature hath placed in our
power." He affirmed that "we shall not fight our battles
alone. There is a just God who presides over the destinies
of nations, and who will raise up friends to fight our battles
for us." And to the question, "Is life so dear, or peace so
sweet, as to be purchased at the price of chains and slavery?"
the answer came, "Forbid it, Almighty God!"[8] The Continental Congress's declaration of July 6, 1775, was likewise
filled with references to "the divine Author of our existence,"
"reverence for our great Creator," "the Divine favour towards
us," and "those powers, which our beneficent Creator hath

---

7. *Ibid.*, p. 92.
8. Moses Coit Tyler, *Patrick Henry* (Ithaca: Cornell University Press,
1962), pp. 144-145.

graciously bestowed upon us," before closing with an expression of "humble confidence in the mercies of the supreme and impartial Judge and Ruler of the Universe."[9] The shape of the religious aspects of Congress's declaration of 1775 was perhaps atypical for the colonists in general since it was largely a product of Thomas Jefferson's perception of God and religious truth, but the general religious tone of the resolutions was most characteristic of colonial reactions to the move for independence.

The injection of religious concerns into the Revolutionary discussion, even if it was not always in direct support of the Patriotic cause, was widespread. As there was much argument concerning the wisdom of the Revolutionary course, so was there a variety of ways in which religious perspectives were applied to the Revolutionary debate. American society in the mid-eighteenth century was, to a much greater degree than in England, still suffused with a religious spirit. Even among those who had left behind the dogmas of Orthodox Protestantism, the values and attitudes of that belief system continued to exert considerable influence. For the very many colonials who still advocated and practiced one of the several varieties of traditional Christianity, religious perceptions were involved willy-nilly with the Revolutionary arguments and the political crises leading to the war.

The series of evangelical awakenings, beginning in the late 1720's and continuing in certain areas into the 1750's and known in its most concentrated aspect as the Great Awakening, further reasserted the religious perspective in the Revolutionary generation. Unlike England, where the revivals of the eighteenth century had only marginal effect on the English centers of power, the effects of the revival in America were pervasive. While it would not be until the turn of the nineteenth century that evangelicalism in England would have an overt and visible impact on the course of English political life, most spectacularly in bringing an end to the slave trade, the effects of the Great Awakening were felt immediately in the colonies.

---

9. *Documents of American History,* Vol. I, 92, 95.

Even granting the general colonial preoccupation with liberty and rights, it is not possible to assess adequately the nature of Christian responses to the Revolutionary crisis without a grasp of the general religious history of the colonies in the eighteenth century. The ideology undergirding revolt against Great Britain was persuasive, and it influenced the thinking of colonial Christians, but by itself it does not account for the ways in which believers rose to the challenge of revolution. Only a grasp of general religious history in colonial America and, particularly, of the religious ferment in the mid-eighteenth century will provide the necessary background for illuminating Christian attitudes to the logic and practice of rebellion.

II   *The Religious Background*

The story of religion in the American colonies is the story of Puritanism. Even where the specific categories of covenantal theology or the lifestyle of the Bible commonwealths did not prevail, a distinctly Puritan ethos exerted its sway. Historians of early America, both of its religious and secular aspects, have agreed concerning the prominence of the Puritan strain in the nation's early history. Sydney E. Ahlstrom, in his *Religious History of the American People,* speaks of the "dominance of Puritanism in the American religious heritage." He further maintains that

> the future United States was settled and to a large degree shaped by those who brought with them a very special form of radical Protestantism which combined a strenuous moral precisionism, a deep commitment to evangelical experientialism, and a determination to make the state responsible for the support of these moral and religious ideas.[1]

Speaking more directly of the American Revolution, one of the most respected historians of colonial America, Edmund S. Morgan, has claimed that

> the movement in all its phases, from the resistance against Parliamentary taxation in the 1760's to the establishment of a national government and national

1. Sydney E. Ahlstrom, *A Religious History of the American People* (New Haven: Yale University Press, 1972), p. 1090.

policies in the 1790's was affected, not to say guided, by a set of values inherited from the age of puritanism.[2]

The extent of this Puritan influence is indicated by the fact that approximately three-fourths of the colonists at the time of the Revolution were identified with denominations that had arisen from the Reformed, Puritan wing of European Protestantism: Congregationalism, Presbyterianism, Baptists, German and Dutch Reformed.

Difficult as it is to define Puritanism, certain generic qualities can be identified. The Puritan perspective, first of all, saw life as a whole. Puritanism did not separate social, ecclesiastical, and theological concerns. Its comprehensive point of view saw religious significance in public acts and public significance in religious acts. Since good and evil could be readily identified in the affairs of men, barriers between theological judgment and the events of daily life could not be tolerated. Since the battle between good and evil, between God and Satan, was carried into every aspect of life, decisions in the communal life of the wider society had a moral significance equal to those enacted within the narrow confines of the church. Puritanism, in sum, refused to compartmentalize life or exempt non-ecclesiastical affairs from religious scrutiny.

Undergirding the comprehensive scope of Puritan concern were deeply held convictions about God's character and the revelation of himself to men. The Puritan was a strenuous moral athlete because of his vision of God, "a Spirit, infinite, eternal, and unchangeable in His being, wisdom, power, holiness, justice, goodness, and truth."[3] Such a being deserved all the love, dedication, energy, and devotion which the creature, by God's grace, could give back to him. The Puritan, further, believed that the Bible was God's authoritative revelation to mankind and that its pages contained necessary and sufficient guidelines for the proper

2. Edmund S. Morgan, "The Puritan Ethic and the American Revolution," *The William and Mary Quarterly*, 3rd ser., XXIV (January, 1967), 3.
3. *Westminster Shorter Catechism*.

ordering of personal, ecclesiastical, and social life. The elaborate covenantal system with its intricate interweaving of personal salvation, ecclesiastical structure, and political organization was, the Puritan felt, merely the faithful exposition of the divine plan laid out in Scripture. Because God had graciously revealed his will in Scripture, Puritans proceeded with the confidence that every aspect of life could be ordered to the glory of God.

In specific theological terms, Puritanism is part of the Calvinistic or Reformed tradition. Puritans believed that sinful human nature by itself could do nothing spiritually good, that only God's grace in Christ could bring salvation to the sinner, and that without God's supernatural call the sinner would neither desire nor be able to turn from evil to life in God. Puritan theology was not, however, merely an echo of John Calvin's *Institutes,* for English and American Puritans read and appropriated the whole range of sixteenth-century reformers, among whom Calvin was a notable, but by no means the ultimate, authority.

The distinguishing characteristic of Puritanism was its effort to unite the principles of Reformation Christianity and a comprehensive view of the world. From the testimony of the continental reformers and their own study of Scripture, the Puritans were convinced that a vital personal religion was the wellspring of all earthly good. They were equally convinced that all aspects of life, whether political, social, cultural, economic, or ecclesiastical, needed to be brought into subjection to God. This Puritan synthesis of heart religion and comprehensive concern for all areas of life drew upon the continental Reformed heritage but was, in its fullest expression, the unique contribution of the English-speaking Reformation to the Christian world.

Puritanism, finally, constituted a dissenting element in English religious history. As a consequence, the issue of freedom was never far from view. The early settlers of Massachusetts did, in a genuine sense, come to the New World to worship freely, even if their conception of freedom was markedly different from that which gained prominence in the colonies before the Revolution. The freedom which early New England sought was the liberty to pursue truth unfettered by the dumb dogs and hirelings of the English establishment. Those who could not agree with New England's leaders concerning the nature of that "truth" were "free" to move on to uninhabited regions of the New World. If, by the time of the Revolution, freedom had begun to assume its modern definition of unencumbered choice among various options *within* a single society, this does not negate the fact that freedom, however defined, had been a major concern for Puritans throughout their history in the New World.

American Puritanism, even in this generic sense, was never wholly without rivals in the colonies and, hence, never without the tempering which the presence of such rivals demanded. From the earliest days of colonization, some members of the Church of England in the colonies resisted the Puritan ethos. By the eighteenth century, the Puritan strain within that communion had largely been replaced by the establishmentarian outlook prevailing within the eighteenth-century church in England. Although their numbers were small, Roman Catholics, Lutherans, and German pietists had also established a foothold in the colonies by the eighteenth century. In addition, dissenters from the dissenting Puritans themselves, such as the Quakers, exerted an influence at cross purposes with certain aspects of the dominant Puritan outlook in the colonies.

The character of the Puritan influence in the colonies is more clearly seen when the regions within the English possessions — New England, middle, and southern colonies — are distinguished. In New England, Congregationalism dominated numerically and culturally. Although their own feisty progeny, the Separates and the Baptists, provided strong competition in the eighteenth century, Congregationalists defined the moral tone and the religious outlook of that region at the time of the Revolution and well beyond. The Puritan strain was also strong in the middle colonies but without the institutional control which the established Congregational churches in New England possessed. Although Presbyterians and the Dutch Reformed exerted considerable influence in New York, the Church of England was legally established in the colony's lower counties, and New York City's cosmopolitan character prevented any one group from gaining religious dominance. William Penn's policy of religious toleration opened Pennsylvania to Lutheran, pietistic, and Presbyterian interests, as well as providing a base for the strongest Quaker community in the New World. This diversity, in spite of early Quaker preeminence, insured that no one denomination would control Pennsylvania's religious affairs.

In the southern colonies, Puritan influence until the mid-eighteenth century was almost exclusively a matter of atmosphere rather than explicit theological conviction. Although Virginia's earliest settlers had been heavily influenced by Puritanism, the colony's Anglican establishment by the end of the seventeenth century reflected the broad, nondogmatic, anti-enthusiastic religion of England's established church. The Church of England was also established in the other southern colonies, but it provided little encouragement to the type of theological and moral exertions characteristic of colonies to the north. In Maryland, the Catholic influence dating from the founding Calvert family had been blunted but still exerted a force in counteraction to Puritanism.

The chronology of eighteenth-century American religion, like its geography, is also divisible into three distinct units: the period before the Great Awakening, the revival itself, and the period following. The years before the revival were marked by strains and tensions within colonial religious life. In Massachusetts, for example, the turn of the eighteenth century witnessed several disquieting encroachments against the comprehensive New England Way. During the seventeenth century the Puritan leaders had laid great stress on both sincere personal religion and effective, if unofficial, control of society and politics by religious interests. But now a new church in Boston, the Brattle Street congregation, ignored the old way of admitting its members without a specific confession of Christian experience. The leading minister in the Connecticut River Valley, Solomon Stoddard of Northampton, posed a similar threat to the well-ordered system of earlier days by loosening bars to attendance at the Lord's Supper. The most respected defender of the old New England Way, Increase Mather, feared that the actions of Stoddard and the Brattle Street church would dilute the spirituality of New England's churches to such an extent that they could no longer perform their sanctifying function in Massachusetts society. The influence of old ways was also being attacked at Harvard, where Mather was being eased out of his position as president. To add insult to injury, Increase's son, Cotton, was coming under fire for the part he had played in the Salem witch trials of the previous decade.

Nor did the tensions ease up in Massachusetts as the century wore on. Conscientious citizens wondered what was to be done with the increasingly prosperous and self-sufficient merchants who insisted on approaching economic and political problems in the colony without specific reference to religion or the principles underlying the New England heritage. They searched in vain for evidences of the sincere heart religion which had animated the founders. And they could not see how the community could tolerate the kind of disrespectful satire directed at ecclesiastical and political leaders by such upstarts as James Franklin and his younger brother, Benjamin. Secular concerns seemed to leave no room for religion, true godliness was on the wane, and the community, with all that it implied to Puritanism, seemed about to fall apart in pursuit of worldly gain.

If the tensions early in the century were not felt so keenly in the middle and southern colonies, they were nonetheless present. Heavy migrations from Ulster, the Palatinate, and England itself combined with the fecundity of earlier settlers to foster rapid growth and an undisciplined frontier atmosphere in many parts of the middle colonies. Ministers were in short supply, and pioneering farmers, beset by Indians and the rigors of the wilderness, seemed to have little taste or time for religion. In Philadelphia, the Quakers grew in number, wealth, and power, but decreased in spiritual ardor and evangelistic zeal. In Frederick B. Tolles' apt phrase, their concerns were beginning to shift from the

meetinghouse to the countinghouse.[4] In the southern colonies, fluctuations in tobacco prices and the caprices of
nature brought some men to ruin and raised up others to
wealth. The Church of England, established in name, lacked
an efficient hierarchy. James Blair filled the post of colonial
commissary with distinction for over half a century, but
his efforts could not compensate for the lack of a bishop
in the colonies since, particularly in Virginia, local vestries
made up of the leading landowners exercised nearly complete
control over ecclesiastical affairs. Like its mother country,
Virginia's religious life during the early eighteenth century
was marked by an absence of spiritual zeal and a lack of
concern for bringing religion to bear on day-to-day activities.

The Great Awakening did not spring fully armed
from the brow of Jonathan Edwards as some would have it
today, nor was it a well-organized, chronologically discrete
event like modern revivals. It was rather a gradual and pervasive turn to religion which took up and reemphasized certain elements in the Puritan heritage, proclaimed them with
a new and compelling urgency, and in its wake left American
society and the Puritan heritage itself markedly changed.
With some legitimacy it may be said to have continued for
twenty-five years, although the most notable manifestations
in any one area were invariably confined to much shorter
periods. Its active life extended from the late 1720's when
Theodore Frelinghuysen began to decry the hypocrisy of
ecclesiastical formalism and to preach the necessity of heart
religion to his Dutch Reformed congregation in Raritan,
New Jersey, at least until the founding of Baptist churches
in North Carolina in 1755. Its great peaks were George
Whitefield's preaching tour in New England during the fall
of 1740 and the literary works of Jonathan Edwards which
described and defended the theology and practice of the
revival. Its valleys included the waves of ecclesiastical schism
and the unrestrained ravings of spiritual fanatics such as
James Davenport who tried to out-Whitefield Whitefield.

---

4. Frederick B. Tolles, *Meeting House and Counting House: The
Quaker Merchants of Colonial Philadelphia, 1682-1763* (Chapel Hill:
University of North Carolina Press, 1948).

After the revival — and the revival ended at different times and in different ways throughout the colonies — the religious landscape was changed forever. Old ways had both come under attack and acquired new defenders, many had left the established churches to chart their own spiritual paths, new groups capitalizing upon the revival's thought and methodology grew rapidly, and ideas cast up by the Awakening led to new departures in theology. Concepts prominent in the revival also provided the public arena with bold new metaphors which political and social movements were able to turn to their own advantage. In short, the period after the Great Awakening was a time in which the principles of the revival were being digested, rejected, developed, opposed, expanded, or transformed. While the Awakening itself did not always answer the questions or solve the difficulties which had troubled religious America before its occurrence, it did alter forever the shape of the problems and bequeath to the next era new ways to come to grips with them.

The comprehensive character of the revival is seen most clearly in its effects on the churches, its penetration of class barriers, and its effect upon public figures not usually figuring in colonial religious history.

In the churches of the Puritan heritage, the revival thrust up questions of theology, forced a reexamination of the basis for ecclesiastical fellowship, and called the value of certain religious traditions into question. Churches beyond the Puritan pale also felt the revival's effect. The Church of England, for example, was forced to reexamine its own methods and beliefs in light of the intense religious concern active in society at large. In some places, such as the Anglican church in New Jersey which welcomed Whitefield and maintained good relations with evangelistic Presbyterians and Methodists throughout the eighteenth century, Anglicans participated directly in the revival of religion. More commonly, as in Massachusetts, the Church of England became a haven for those offended by the revival's upsetting progress. Baptists in the colonies, although not immediately involved in the first stages of the revival, were among its

principal benefactors. They provided an appealing alternative
to those who rejected what they considered the second-class,
birthright religion of the established communions.

Nor was the Great Awakening limited to the
lower classes or the socially dispossessed. The first Boston
minister to correspond with Whitefield was the venerable
Dr. Benjamin Colman, dean of Boston's ministers and pastor
of the very Brattle Street church whose founding some forty
years earlier had so disturbed the ecclesiastical orthodox in
Massachusetts. Dr. Colman, who had overseen the growth
of Brattle Street to a large and prestigious church, welcomed
Whitefield and did not consider it beneath the dignity of his
position to actively support the revival. Students and tutors
at Yale and Harvard were swept off their feet by Whitefield's message in the early 1740's, many of them abandon-
ing their studies to embark on satellite preaching tours. Not
until Whitefield published his opinion that the colleges' "Light
is become Darkness, Darkness that may be felt, and is complained of by the most godly Ministers,"[5] did Yale and
Harvard withdraw their support.

The revival also touched public figures not particularly well known for their religious activities. Benjamin
Franklin, by now transplanted to Philadelphia, was fasci-
nated, if not convinced, by Whitefield's preaching and was
his printer in Philadelphia for a number of years. At least
two of the Revolution's most conspicuous firebrands were
also pulled into the revival's sway. Samuel Adams is said
to have turned frequently to the works of Jonathan Edwards
as a source of spiritual refreshment, and young Patrick
Henry was deeply influenced by the ministry of Samuel
Davies, the Presbyterian awakener of Virginia.

Another way of coming to terms with the Great
Awakening is to examine the men who seemed to embody
it, George Whitefield and Jonathan Edwards. Both were
figures of controversy in their age; both deserve recognition as memorable figures in an age saturated with great
men. Whitefield sparked religiously desiccated sensibilities

---

5. Edwin Scott Gaustad, *The Great Awakening in New England* (Chicago: Quadrangle Books, 1968), p. 30.

and became an effective champion of heart religion. His re-markable energy, his ecclesiastical catholicity, and his spec-tacular oratorical gifts made him without question the "Grand Itinerant." As merely one indication of his dedi-cation and appeal, it has been determined that during his first week in Boston in 1740, from Friday, September 19 to the following Thursday, he preached at least ten times to crowds ranging up to 8,000 listeners. He considered no pulpit, no village square, no public facility beneath his dignity as a place to proclaim the gospel. Even those who could not subscribe to his message found its presentation captivating. Benjamin Franklin wrote that Whitefield's "every accent, every emphasis, every modulation of the voice, was so perfectly well tuned and well placed, that, without being interested in the subject, one could not help being pleased with the discourse."[6] Those who subscribed to his message spoke more simply of "Mr. Whitefield's Plain, Powerful, and Awakening Preaching."[7]

Notwithstanding the impact of Whitefield, if the revival had not gone beyond spectacular itineration and violent conversions, it would not have penetrated the American consciousness as deeply as it did. Beside the public performances, the revival also produced a flood of literature in which the writings of Jonathan Edwards are paramount. Edwards' *Narrative of Surprising Conversions,* published first in 1736 as a letter to Dr. Colman describing a 1734 revival in Edwards' own Northampton, delineated the psychology of conversion that would dominate the Great Awakening and, to a certain extent, the evangelistic tradition in the United States to this very day. In 1743 he published *Some Thoughts Concerning the Present Revival of Religion in New England.* This volume, while admitting that excesses did attend certain aspects of the Awakening, maintained that God was at work in the colonies and that all true Chris-tians should welcome this divine activity. *Religious Affec-tions* (1746) completed his analysis of the revival by de-

---

6. *Ibid.,* p. 29.
7. *Ibid.*

scribing meticulously the differences between those emotions which indicated the presence of a regenerate condi-
tion and those which did not. The more overtly theological
and philosophical treatises of his later career, *Freedom of
Will* (1754), *Original Sin* (1758), and the posthumous *Nature of True Virtue* (1765) were both apologies for the
strict Calvinism which Edwards saw as undergirding the
revival and accounts of how God's goodness and glory were
reflected in the lives of authentic believers. In these works
Edwards not only provided a systematic rationale for the
religiosity of the Awakening but also set out an interpretation of historic Calvinism with which academic theologians
continue to wrestle in our own time.

The Great Awakening, then, was important for
its broad scope in the colonies as well as for the dynamism
and influence of its leaders, most notably Whitefield and
Edwards. As difficult as it is to define Puritanism, it is only
slightly less difficult to define the Great Awakening which
revitalized and, at the same time, altered that Puritan heritage. To answer the question, What in fact was the Great
Awakening? at least four distinct viewpoints must be considered: its relation to the comprehensive model of church
and society inherited from Puritanism, its theological and
ecclesiastical contributions, its examination of the morality
of personal actions, and its methods and preaching practices.

Faced with the two parts of the Puritan synthesis,
personal religion and a comprehensive vision of society, the
awakeners opted unreservedly for personal religion. Whitefield directed his preaching at the individual heart; Edwards
examined the religious processes within individuals. The
awakeners were not socially callous as modern evangelists
are often portrayed, for they too sought the good of society.
In their eyes, however, societal good was a function of personal virtue, personal godliness, and personal deeds mani-
festing the goodness of God. Society, they felt, must indeed
be transformed by the gospel, but this transformation had
to proceed from the supernatural act of God in renewing
the individual. People were called first to seek the Kingdom
of God: only then could all else be added unto them.

The central theological principles of the revival were familiar to most colonists. The awakeners expounded on the holiness of God, the sinfulness of men, and the futility of seeking salvation through any means but the freely offered grace of God in Jesus Christ. The special attraction of these time-honored doctrines in the 1730's and 1740's owed much to the immediacy and vividness with which they were preached. Edwards, for example, in sermons preached between 1734 and 1741, justified the future punishment of the wicked by holding the evil of sinners up against "the honor and glory of the infinite God." He described the evil of unregenerate men as so great that "if God should let you go, you would immediately sink and swiftly descend and plunge into the bottomless gulf." But he also reminded his hearers that: "There meet in Jesus Christ, infinite justice and infinite grace. . . . Though his justice be so strict with respect to all sin, and every breach of the law, yet he has grace sufficient for every sinner, and even the chief of sinners."[8] The effectiveness of such preaching owed much also to the receptivity of the audiences. When a sinner felt that God had graciously rescued him from the just deserts of his evil nature, the terrifying sense of sin was overmastered by an even greater sense of beatitude.

The intensity with which this release from sin was felt had serious implications for local churches. If God was as inimical to evil as the awakeners claimed, was it not folly to allow individuals into the church who could not testify convincingly that they were saved by grace? The halfway practice of church membership, dating back three-fourths of a century or more in New England, had long allowed the children of baptized members to assume a half membership so long as they affirmed the orthodox doctrines and kept themselves from conspicuous scandal. The children of the revival, in reaction to this practice, argued vociferously that mere intellectual assent to Christian beliefs and mere freedom from scandal were not sufficient indications that a person was a child of God. They claimed that even the

---

8. Jonathan Edwards, *Selections,* ed. Clarence H. Faust and Thomas H. Johnson (New York: Hill & Wang, 1962), pp. 150, 162, and 123.

devil himself believed the creed and could present an out-wardly upright demeanor. While the awakened did not aban-don the criteria of orthodox belief and a decorous life, they went on to demand as a further criterion for membership a credible profession of Christian faith, i.e., a testimony to the work of the Holy Spirit in the life. The doubters might scorn this demand as enthusiasm, but the children of the revival knew that the church of God must strive for the same corporate purity that marked the soul renewed by redeeming grace.

The initial success of the revival also led to a greater emphasis on eschatological matters. During the first bloom of the revival it seemed possible that the earthly Kingdom of God prophesied in Scripture might become a reality as more and more sinners turned in repentance and faith to Christ. Millennialism, the belief that there will be a literal thousand-year reign of Christian peace on the earth before the end of the world, was not a new doctrine to New England, but the revival changed the perspective in which this coming millennium was viewed. At the turn of the eighteenth century, Cotton Mather had described a millennium which would arise with the cataclysmic return of Christ after a gradual sinking of the world into sin. After the successes of the Great Awakening, Mather's pessimism was replaced by a generally more optimistic viewpoint. Many thought it likely that the gospel would now advance by the preaching of the Word and the work of the Holy Spirit until the whole world was Christianized and the nations joined in peaceful worship and obedience to God. The con-viction that America might be the fountainhead of this last push to the millennium increased as the revival flourished; it did not diminish even when the startling successes had become things of the past.

The Great Awakening, which stressed the grace of God so strongly, did not neglect the importance of be-havior as an indication of internal spiritual conditions. While admitting that hypocrites could imitate the Christian life for a period of time, the awakeners also taught that no true change of heart could exist without a life of public goodness.

Edwards himself provided the classic formulation of this belief in his *Treatise Concerning Religious Affections*. As opposed to the false manifestations of Christianity, vacuous emotionalism tinged with Christian coloring and nominally religious formalism,

> gracious and holy affections have their exercise and fruit in Christian practice. I mean, they have that influence and power upon him who is the subject of 'em, that they cause that a practice, which is universally conformed to, and directed by Christian rules, should be the practice and business of his life.[9]

The effort to restrict church membership to the elect gained strength from this teaching, for an individual's behavior as well as his confession could be examined for signs of true conversion. Tendencies toward antinomianism in the revival were blunted, if not altogether eliminated, by this emphasis, for no individual could logically claim to be a child of God while treating the law of God with disrespect or disdain. This aspect of the Awakening refocused the Puritan emphasis on the comprehensiveness of divine imperatives by asserting that every aspect of life was capable of religious significance. Thus, the vigorous moralism that is associated in the popular mind today with Puritanism in truth owes as much to the Awakening as to the Puritan heritage from which the Awakening arose.

Finally, the Awakening's methodology reasserted the importance of emotion in religious matters. While Edwards and other champions of the revival wielded logic skillfully, they did not assume that true Christianity was, in the last analysis, a matter of ratiocination or reflection. They urged men to fear for their sins before God and to seek his mercy with their whole hearts. The call of the Awakening was not to reflection and decorum but to feeling and action. Where sermons in the early eighteenth century had customarily been closely argued treatises read from written manuscripts,

---

9. Jonathan Edwards, *Religious Affections,* ed. John E. Smith (New Haven: Yale University Press, 1959), p. 383.

Whitefield and the other itinerants moved people by exciting extemporaneous sermons that drove home simple themes with zeal and vigor. The awakeners, who themselves had known the urgent need to make peace with God and the only slightly less urgent desire to reflect godliness in their daily lives, forsook the forms of religion as they had been handed down to them. Not contemplation but action, not assent but conversion, was their goal.

The effects of the Great Awakening ranged widely. In the first place, the revival drastically altered the ecclesiastical landscape. Among the heirs of the Puritans, where differences of opinion had once coexisted in uneasy peace under a common set of professed convictions, distinct parties emerged. The classic statements of Edwards became the watchwords of a New Divinity group. The adherents of this party remained within Presbyterianism and established Congregationalism, but they did not moderate their proclamation that God must be sovereign in conversion and that the churches must be purified of all but the professedly regenerate.

To the left of these Edwardseans, more radical New Lights (as the advocates of the revival in general were called) abandoned the established churches in order to seek the purity of the gospel in "Separate" assemblies. Many of these more radical New Lights, such as Isaac Backus, would soon become Baptists, convinced that baptism of adult believers was the proper way of testifying to the saving work of God in the life.

On the other side of the Edwardsean New Divinity a group arose which was uneasy with the supernaturalism, the emotionalism, and the enthusiasm of the revival. This party's longtime spokesman, Charles Chauncy of Boston's First Church, sounded the call to resistance in his *Seasonable Thoughts on the State of Religion in New England,* published in 1743. This work attacked the emotionalism and irresponsibility of the revival and revealed its author's predilection for an enlightened rationalism that stressed human capabilities and de-emphasized the active work of God in the world. Although the members of this group, called the Old Lights, were known as the theological liberals of that day, their social and political views were frequently allied with established colonial interests.

The last group was referred to as Old Calvinists or as moderate Old Lights. With the theological liberals they shared a distaste for the social upheaval occasioned by the revival, but they also cherished a Puritan orthodoxy similar to that held by the New Lights. Ezra Stiles, president of Yale College from 1778 to 1795, was representative of this group. Broad-minded and tolerant by the standards of his day, he rejected the theological dogmatism and evangelistic fervor of the New Light as well as the disorder which the revival and theological controversy had wrought in colonial society. On the other hand, however, he was also uneasy with the drift toward rationalism that characterized theological opposition to the revival. These Old Calvinists were, hence, men in the ecclesiastical middle. As the century wore on, they either accustomed themselves to the social excesses of the New Lights in order to cling to their theological heritage or modified the content of that heritage to preserve the social and ecclesiastical stability which the Old Lights defended.

The fragmentation of the Puritan monolith into discernible parties also provided more room for countervailing religious groups in the colonies. For Anglicans, Roman Catholics, Quakers, Lutherans, and German pietists, Puritanism no longer exerted such a uniform impression upon intellectual matters or on the culture in general. Beyond the freer rein provided for non-Puritan groups, the Awakening's theological teachings further weakened traditional religious structures in the colonies. Some of the hierarchical authoritarianism latent in the Puritanism of the seventeenth century gave way before the renewed application of the Calvinistic doctrines of predestination, free grace, and the inability of place or station to insure salvation. A well-known sermon by Gilbert Tennent, who pioneered the revival among Presbyterians in New Jersey, on "The Dangers of an Unconverted Ministry" showed the direction in which these Calvinistic doctrines could lead. If conversion was the overwhelming precondition for authority in the churches, then ecclesiastical office and social prominence were no longer as important as the spiritual status which God could grant to any man regardless of his station in life.

The Awakening also exercised considerable influence on the shape of colonial society in less clearly ecclesiastical ways. It tended to break down the provincialism of the various colonies and to aid in the process of inter-colonial communication which would one day lead to the formation of *united* states. From Charlestown to Boston, Whitefield's name was in the air. However men differed on the value of his work, he provided a unifying point of inter-colonial concern. The "melting pot" effect of the revival is illustrated by the career of Gilbert Tennent. Born in Ireland, educated by his father in Bedford, New York, and a recipient of a master's degree from Yale College in Connecticut, he pastored a Presbyterian church in New Brunswick, New Jersey. His congregation, which included many settlers from New England, could read in the papers of its minister's revivalistic labors in such faraway places as Piscataqua, Maine, or Hanover County, Virginia. Given this trans-colonial spiritual vision, the pressure on Tennent and his congregation to consider themselves American Christians instead of merely New Jersey Presbyterians was strong indeed.

The Awakening, by emphasizing the importance of doctrine, convictions, and ideological thinking, also reasserted the importance of ideas for private action and public policy. From their understanding of cardinal religious truths, the awakeners called on people to make significant personal choices and to alter their modes of life. Opponents of the revival were also challenged to justify their opposition and their own ecclesiastical practices through appeal to a system of belief. At least partially as a heritage from the Great Awakening, colonists in the mid-eighteenth century were attuned to the implications of ideas and convinced that different courses of action could be condemned or pursued because of their relationship to well-defined ideologies.

As an outgrowth of this conviction, the Awakening focused attention on the nature of virtue, both public and private. Social and political problems were not just idle curiosities but opportunities to apply truth to life. If God were as powerful and all-comprehending as the awakeners claimed, there was no aspect of life which could be excluded from the application of his law. Sensitivities to moral questions and the ethics of personal actions were heightened as a result of the Awakening much as in the present day the nation's moral consciousness has been raised by the Watergate scandal.

These effects of the Awakening must be taken into account in tracing the growth of Revolutionary sentiment, for at a very early stage eddies from the revival mingled with other currents in the intellectual and social life of the colonies. The revival, in fact, reawakened interest in concepts which bore directly on political and social questions. Freedom was again a byword. To Isaac Backus and the Baptists, participation in an established church that was maintained legally and financially by the official government of a colony was impossible. The essence of Christianity, Backus contended, was to be found in the uncoerced acts of benevolence which flowed by nature, and not by externally imposed sanctions, from a heart that had been reborn. Just as official laws and rules could not produce the new birth, so the new birth could not bear proper fruit in a system of ecclesiastical coercion. The concept of a millennium on earth which the revival resuscitated also bore fruit in a quasi-public way. It gave fresh expression to the ancient longing for a golden age of truth, virtue, and prosperity as well as to the self-satisfying conviction that such a golden age would arise as a result of concentrated national effort.

In raising these kinds of ideas, hopes, and expectations, the revivalists themselves acted with scant regard to political consequences. These themes, nevertheless, had political implications which would be of greatest importance during the controversy with Great Britain. Puritanism had by its very nature embraced a political outlook, and the Puritan element in America, revived and expanded by the Great Awakening, did not disassociate itself from the politics of revolution.

The ways in which religion interacted with the Revolution will be examined at greater length later, but some of the more prominent aspects of the relationship may be mentioned here. In the first instance, the Puritan heritage saw to it that the politics of English-colonial difficulties assumed a moral dimension. Given the Puritan concern for the religious implications of public acts and the Awakening's increased stress on virtue as a mark of regeneration, official venality and malfeasance in office took on cosmic ethical overtones. "Liberty" and "freedom" became not merely operative social principles but rallying cries expressed in religious terms and fraught with spiritual implications. Social problems, whether affecting the imperial connection or merely within the colonies, likewise could not escape the comprehensive spirituality which prevailed in the political perceptions of colonial Christians.

Secondly, because the Awakening had dislocated as well as revived the religious connection in America, there was no single, unified application of ethical and religious categories to the Revolutionary conflict. Various responses were made to the crisis of the Revolution within the Puritan heritage itself, not even to speak of the actions within such bodies as the Anglicans or Lutherans. While all groups acted on political and constitutional questions at least partially from moral and religious grounds, they did not always share identical analyses of the problems or agree as to the best solutions.

Thirdly, as a factor of particular importance, the problem of the Church of England became not simply a matter for ecclesiastical discernment but for general political discussion. Since the Church of England was perceived as an agent of official British policy, its fate was linked to the success of that policy in the colonies. If Great Britain were a general threat to divinely ordained privileges, then the Church of England had to be resisted as a particular threat to colonial life as a whole rather than just a competing denomination.

Finally, the political prospects of a new age in which freedom and prosperity reigned shared the millennial overtones of the revival. It took little effort to secularize the revivalists' spiritual vision in order to accommodate the political aspirations of a vigorous colonial people forced to break away from their mother country because of what they saw as the latter's irredeemable corruption.

While it is important not to forget other factors which went into the formation of Christian responses to the Revolutionary crisis, it is necessary to remember that the Great Awakening was the most important and enduring religious phenomenon in eighteenth-century America. Ministers and other religiously active individuals approached the war with perspectives that had been developed while supporting, accommodating, or opposing the revival. As we examine the different ways in which Christians in the colonies responded to the Revolutionary crisis, it will be necessary to remember that the dominant Puritan heritage in America, and more particularly the events of the Great Awakening, had shaped religious life in the colonies. For better or for worse, political events were going to be viewed through religious spectacles. Political and religious ideologies were not preserved in hermetically sealed compartments. Much to the contrary: as Christians had thought and acted on religious matters, so would they in large measure think and act in the Revolutionary struggle.

III The Patriotic Response

Throughout the Revolutionary period, colonial min-
isters labored diligently to bring Christian truths to bear on
the momentous issues embroiling the British colonies. From
1750, when Jonathan Mayhew of Boston expounded Romans
13 to defend the people's right to revolt when their rulers
did not govern for their good, to 1783, when Ezra Stiles
described the blessings promised to Israel in Deuteronomy
26:19 as "allusively prophetic of the future prosperity and
splendor of the United States," religious energies stimulated,
sanctioned, and supported the movement for American independence.[1] Although the practice of analyzing public events
in terms of God's special dealings with the colonies had
been commonplace in early American Puritanism, it was not
until the imperial wars with France that this practice began
to take on the nationalistic tone which would characterize
the Revolutionary era. When, for example, Quebec fell to
British forces in 1759, Solomon Williams, a cousin of Jonathan Edwards and the minister of Lebanon, Connecticut,
discussed the great victory and its significance for the colonists by a direct application of Exodus 15:2 to the American
situation: "The Lord is my strength and song, and he is

---

1. Jonathan Mayhew, *A Discourse Concerning Unlimited Submission
and Non-Resistance to the Higher Powers* ... (Boston: D. Fowle, 1750);
Ezra Stiles, *The United States elevated to Glory and Honor* ... (1783),
in *The Pulpit of the American Revolution: or, the Political Sermons
of the Period of 1776,* ed. John Wingate Thornton (Boston: Gould &
Lincoln, 1860), p. 403.

become my salvation: he is my God, and I will prepare him a habitation; my father's God, and I will exalt him."

After the French and Indian War, during which Americans had exulted in the glories of British liberty, the new imperial policies caused a shift in colonial thinking. In light of Great Britain's apparent disregard for colonial happiness, many of the colonists now felt that the gravest threat to personal liberty and social well-being arose not from infidel, papist France but from a corrupt and morally degenerate England. Christian leaders also cast a wary eye upon British encroachments. When it became evident to many colonists that Parliament's oppressive measures were a product of the vicious, anti-Christian nature of British society, ministers felt no qualms about using religion to justify colonial resistance. After the Stamp Act had been passed by Parliament but before it had been implemented in the colonies, Jonathan Mayhew preached on Galatians 5:12-13, with special reference to the phrase "ye have been called unto liberty." To Mayhew it was obvious that the stamp tax reduced the colonies to slavery, the very antithesis of the liberty proclaimed by Paul in his epistle to the Galatians. When the repeal of the Stamp Act in 1766 seemed to presage a restored era of good feeling between Britain and her colonies, Charles Chauncy of Boston used the words of Proverbs 25:25 to hail the repeal as "good news from a far country." This praise for a British action proved, however, to be a momentary aberration in the colonial attitude toward the imperial connection, for as the political crisis mounted, so did Christian support of the Patriot cause. Even someone like Isaac Backus, the New Light Baptist whose doubts about the drift of Patriotic thought are discussed in the next chapter, sounded a clear call for united colonial resistance on the Sunday immediately following the battles of Lexington and Concord. His text was I Chronicles 12:32: "And ... the children of Issachar ... were men that had understanding of the times, to know what Israel ought to do." None of Backus' listeners had any doubt about the identity of the true sons of Issachar in colonial America in 1775, nor did they question what now needed to be done to Great Britain.

Christian encouragement of the Patriot cause and, more significantly, support of the political ideology underlying resistance to Britain were not limited to any one social stratum nor to any one of the major theological groupings emerging from the Great Awakening. Charles Chauncy of Boston's prestigious First Church heartened his auditors in 1770 by applying Psalm 22:4, "Our fathers trusted in thee; they trusted, and thou didst deliver them," to the oppressive maneuvers of the royal governor. Three years later Benjamin Trumbull of tiny North Haven, Connecticut, expounded Exodus 1:8, "Now there arose up a new king over Egypt, which knew not Joseph," in defense of the proposition that the artificial imposition of foreign officials upon a self-sufficient people led to ruin and corruption. As an indication of the spread of Patriotic Whiggery throughout the theological spectrum, it is interesting to note that in the perilous year of 1776 both Old Lights and New Lights interpreted John's prophecies in the book of Revelation in the same way. In that year the theologically liberal Samuel West of Dartmouth, Massachusetts, and the conservative Samuel Sherwood of Weston, Connecticut, both described British oppression in terms of the beast of Revelation 13.

Christians did not, as has been too often assumed by historians of the Revolution, support the Patriot cause universally or without mental and moral reservations. As subsequent chapters will show, significant numbers of American believers questioned specific aspects or the entirety of the drive for independence and of the ideology fueling that drive. Nevertheless, it is true that vast numbers of American Christians offered wholehearted support to the movement leading to separation from Great Britain. Certainly the overwhelming majority of clergymen who wrote about the conflict lent Christian support to the Patriot cause. In particular, the direct descendants of Anglo-American Puritanism, Congregationalists and Presbyterians, distinguished themselves in defense of colonial prerogatives. To some observers, in fact, colonial Patriots took on the appearance of religious crusaders. A Hessian captain wrote of his experiences in Pennsylvania, "Call this war . . . by whatever name you may, only call it not an American Rebellion, it is nothing more or less than an Irish-Scotch Presbyterian Rebellion."[2] Joseph Galloway, an influential lawyer from Philadelphia and a speaker of the Pennsylvania provincial legislature before becoming a Loyalist, wrote that when the East India Company secured the tea monopoly, the general insurrection in the colonies was led by "Congregationalists, Presbyterians, and Smugglers."[3] It is important to recognize the kernel of truth in these ejaculations, even if it was expressed through hyperbole: a firm and deep bond did join the Patriotic commitments and the Christian convictions of many Americans.

Recent historical studies of depth and perception have provided much assistance in accounting for this close connection between Christian and Patriotic convictions.[4] While it may be true that some American Christians were merely swept up without reflection in the Patriotic tide, it is also true that deeply held beliefs and attitudes were shared by the Whig and Puritan traditions. American Christians who supported the Patriot cause did so, more often than not, with a deep sense of how profoundly compatible the politics of libertarianism were with the view of the world which had developed in the course of American religious history. Indeed, so deep was the mutual compatibility of late-Puritan Christianity and Whig ideology that over the course of the Revolutionary period it became increasingly difficult to discern where one left off and the other began. The ease with which Whig and Christian thinking merged is at least partially explained by considering several specific themes prominent in both systems.

---

2. In Leonard J. Kramer, "Muskets in the Pulpit, 1776-1783: Part I," *Journal of the Presbyterian Historical Society,* XXXI (December, 1953), 320.
3. In Leonard J. Kramer, "Presbyterians Approach the American Revolution: Part II," *Journal of the Presbyterian Historical Society,* XXXI (September, 1953), 176.
4. See particularly, Alan Heimert, *Religion and the American Mind From the Great Awakening to the Revolution* (Cambridge: Harvard University Press, 1966); and Nathan O. Hatch, *The Sacred Cause of Liberty: Republican Thought and the Millennium in Revolutionary New England* (New Haven: Yale University Press, 1977).

In the first place, the Christian and Whig world views shared what a leading historian of the Revolution has called "a distinctly bearish view of human nature."[5] A century and a half of pulpit oratory had pounded the doctrine of total depravity deep into the New England conscience. Elsewhere in the colonies where the drumbeat of Puritan preaching had not been as steady, colonists still did not harbor a rosy picture of human nature nor gloss over its unlimited capacity for wickedness. Colonists in general knew that without careful scrutiny mankind's inherent bent toward evil would flare repeatedly into the open. While the Whig world view lacked Puritanism's elaborate theological description of human sinfulness, it too cast a jaundiced eye on the innate character of mankind. English Whigs knew only too well how unchecked political power led swiftly to abuses against the persons and property of citizens and how easily well-intentioned men could be sucked into the sinks of intrigue that dominated British politics in the eighteenth century. The transportation of English libertarianism to the colonies had not lessened suspicions concerning the inherently evil propensity of political power in the slightest.

Whigs and Christians also shared a common belief in the mutual interdependence of virtue, freedom, and social well-being. In simplest terms, personal and collective virtue constituted the indispensable foundation for personal liberty and civic health. Liberty in turn was a prerequisite for a decent and honorable society. Tyranny, political oppression, and governmental slavery all reflected the degeneracy of the ruler and spelled distress, corruption, and evil for a society. Without virtue there could be no true liberty; without liberty, no health in society. As early as 1762 this irreducible bond between virtue and liberty had already been well established in the minds of many colonial Christians. In that year Ebenezer Devotion of Windham County, Connecticut, spoke for many of his fellows in proclaiming that the virtue of "fortitude"

---

5. Edmund S. Morgan, *The Birth of the Republic, 1763-89* (Chicago: University of Chicago Press, 1956), p. 6.

had often sav'd a Nation from Tyranny, shook off
the Chains of Slavery, eased their Necks from the
galling Yoke, preserv'd their natural Rights, secur'd
their Liberties as Men, and as Christians, dissipated
a Spirit of Rebellion, and kept them from degenerating
into Beasts.[6]

In the context of the Revolutionary War itself, the connection between this liberty and the well-being of society was
sketched by a New Jersey Presbyterian, Jacob Green, who
believed the free and independent colonies would establish
"the most equitable, rational, natural mode of civil government," end "tyranny and oppression," insure "our natural
rights," and foster prosperity in agriculture, trade and religion.[7]

The virtue which underlay both liberty and a good
society was defined more sharply in negative than in positive terms throughout the eighteenth century. To the Whig,
virtue provided the energy to check the lust for power and
the vigilance to monitor the constant threat of corruption.
For the Christian, to whom virtue had always been involved
in the struggle against sin, it came to include resistance to
threats against the God-given rights of life, liberty, and
property. The positive side of Christian virtue — that is,
righteousness — entailed a right relationship with God, one's
self, and society. While emphasis on personal salvation and
proper Christian living was never entirely displaced during
the Revolutionary age, the weighty political events of the
day focused concern upon the social and military arenas.
Christian virtue, as a consequence, came to be expressed
in increasingly social and political terms even though the
more traditional concerns for personal salvation and sancti-
fication were not neglected.

The banner of freedom around which Christians
and Whigs gathered was woven of varied, yet complementary,

---

6. Ebenezer Devotion, *Fortitude, Love and a Sound Judgment, very
needful Qualifications for the Christian Minister . . .* (New Haven:
James Parker & Co., 1762), p. 10.
7. Jacob Green, *Observations: On the Reconciliation of Great-Britain
and the Colonies . . .* (Philadelphia: Robert Bell, 1776), pp. 19-20, 22,
24, 28-29.

strands. As with the concept of virtue, a strong negative factor was important in the definition of liberty. Puritanism had grown out of a particular understanding of the way in which men were freed *from* sin; the overriding concern of the Whigs was to preserve freedom *from* tyranny. The Reformation's concept of personal freedom from sin was expanded by the Puritans in their effort to also free church and society from the encrustations of institutionalized evil. It was this corporate perspective of Puritanism which merged so neatly with libertarian concerns. The heirs of the Puritans recognized that their efforts to preserve society from sin were very similar to Whig efforts to preserve it from tyranny. Since the Puritan's battle against personal sin was linked tightly with his battle against institutional evil, it was a small, often unconscious step for the Christian to see the personal struggle against sin and the libertarian fight against tyranny as one and the same struggle. Once this link was forged, the fight against British political oppression could be viewed as a fight against sin itself. This series of ideological couplings helps explain some of the apparently disjointed outbursts of the period. To cite just one example, Moses Mather, a Connecticut clergyman whose work we will examine at greater length shortly, was able to use religious language to condemn the Loyalist Governor of Massachusetts, Thomas Hutchinson, for his political errors. Because Hutchinson's political views seemed to violate the standards of Patriotic Whiggery, Mather could contend that his "punishment hereafter, without repentance, must exceed all conception or description."[8]

There was, moreover, an internal and time-honored strain of liberty embedded in the Reformed heritage in America. The most perceptive historian of colonial Presbyterianism has spoken, for example, of "something inherent in Presbyterianism that made the cause of colonial independence congenial to it."[9] Puritan and Reformed bodies in Great

8. Moses Mather, *America's Appeal to the Impartial World . . .* (Hartford: Ebenezer Watson, 1775), p. 60.
9. Leonard J. Trinterud, *The Forming of an American Tradition: A Re-examination of Colonial Presbyterianism* (Philadelphia: Westminster, 1949), p. 251.

Britain had always been dissenting groups. Whether this dissent took the Scottish form of resistance to English ecclesiastical authority or the English form of resistance to the established Anglican church, it had been a persistent theme since the time of the Reformation. The dissenting heritage did not necessarily make Puritan support of the Revolution inevitable, but it did predispose it in that direction.

On a deeper level, the Calvinism to which most Congregationalists and Presbyterians still adhered in the eighteenth century contained several elements which nourished a concern for liberty. God, they felt, possessed unimpeachable freedom to act in grace toward individuals apart from the mediation of priest, prince, or potentate. This way of describing the divine-human relationship inevitably made subjection to authorities in ecclesiastical and political affairs a relative matter. If one's relationship to God was the ultimate concern, and if the establishment of this relationship rested in a sphere beyond human authority, then human authority could never be regarded as absolute or as unequivocally binding. American religious history had witnessed a troublesome application of this type of thinking in the life of Roger Williams. Williams argued early in the seventeenth century that the nature of the gospel was such that external coercion in religious matters inevitably compromised the freedom which true Christianity required. Although such thinking was as destructive of colonial religious establishments as of the Church of England, during the Revolutionary crisis it took on fresh implications for dissenters from the American establishments such as Isaac Backus.

Given the deep and persistent devotion to Christian freedom, it required only a small adjustment to expand concern for the glorious liberty of the children of God into concern for release from British tyranny. The ease with which religiously grounded fears of the Church of England grew into general fear of the British tyrant testifies to the close relation between religious and political freedom in the colonial mind. In the crisis atmosphere of the Revolution the Whig struggle to preserve natural rights and the Christian struggle to protect God-given privileges often became the same thing.

Beyond similar views of human nature and the intimate mutual dependence seen among virtue, liberty, and social good, Christians and Whigs also shared common convictions about the nature of history. Both saw history, in its simplest terms, as a cosmic struggle between the forces of good and the hosts of evil. For the heirs of the Puritans, the struggle between Christ and Antichrist which had raged with particular intensity since the time of the Reformation took on a new urgency in the Revolution. Since the Reformation, Christian commentators had routinely identified the pope as the Antichrist, but as it became clear, particularly during the French and Indian War, that the papacy was but one prominent strand in the fabric of oppression, American Christians increasingly regarded tyranny in general, whether ecclesiastical or political, as the embodiment of Antichrist. This shift brought the Puritan and Whig views of history very close together. To the Whigs, it was apparent that history sketched a repeating cycle of civil rectitude and corruption. Much as Christ had battled Antichrist over the centuries, so moral vigilance had struggled against greed and the grasp for unchecked power. Where probity emerged victorious, nations flourished in material and moral health. But where corruption triumphed, nations suffered severe social and physical reverses.

These viewpoints came together during the Revolutionary period in a uniform attitude toward the early American settlers. Was it not in pursuit of free worship of God that the Puritan founders left the comforts of Old England to flee into a barren and inhospitable wilderness? Were not the corrupt Archbishop Laud and the tyrannical Charles I as responsible in their perverse way for the first Puritan migration as John Winthrop and John Cotton? Although latter-day descendants of these early Puritans tended to overlook the rigor with which the early Puritan settlements enforced their concepts of Christian truth, they did not for a moment doubt that a love of liberty was one of the most

important, if not the supreme, motive for the flight to the
New World.

In a similar merging of Whig and Christian points
of view, both saw an ideal world arising from the Revolutionary struggle for American freedom. The vision of a
fully realized republicanism had long animated proponents
of Whig ideology. It seemed altogether possible that in America, a virgin land where patterns of civic vice and political
corruption had not been engrained as deeply as in Europe,
could emerge a new republic in which men were free and
government nicely balanced. Visions of such an ideal state
had enticed English thinkers since the heady days of the
Puritan Revolution. Some of the fervor in the support of
the American Revolution can be traced to the hope that
this vision could become a reality.

An even older Christian vision added fuel to this
flame. Might it just not be possible, mused the children of
the Puritans, that the millennial age of peace and righteousness foretold in Scripture could be dawning in America.
Particularly when Christian concepts of freedom became
infused with Whig content, the attainment of American
independence seemed linked to the realization of the earthly
Kingdom of God. Millennial thought had always been prominent among the Puritans, even though it was a premillen-
nialism which expected a decline into evil before the coming of the Kingdom that had prevailed earlier in the eighteenth century. Now, however, with the thrilling prospect
of realized (Christian) liberty and the unique opportunity
for virtuous citizens to create their own institutions, it seemed
increasingly likely that the millennial age would arise from
this struggle for liberty and Christianity in which the colonists were engaged. Even before the Declaration of Independence, Ebenezer Baldwin of Danbury, Connecticut, was only
one of the many contemplating the possibility that America
might become "the principal Seat of that glorious Kingdom,
which Christ shall erect upon Earth in the latter Days."[10]

---

10. Ebenezer Baldwin, *The Duty of Rejoicing under Calamities and
Afflictions*... (New York: Hugh Gaine, 1776), p. 38.

In sum, the bond between libertarian ideology and a certain strand of Christian belief was so strong that many defenders of the colonies must properly be labelled Christian Whigs or Whig Christians. The two points of view shared common concerns, distrusted common foes, and defended common liberties. Republican religion, or religious republicanism, was the result. From another perspective, a quasi-Puritan concept of social and religious wholeness seemed to take on new life for some Christians during the Revolutionary period. The old Puritan synthesis of personal religion and comprehensive social involvement had not survived the disruptions and upsets of the early eighteenth century, but a new synthesis in which Puritan elements were still very prominent seemed to lie within the grasp of the Patriotic American Christian.

Like the old Puritan synthesis, Christian libertarianism tended to reduce all religious and political issues to simple moral terms. It continued to emphasize salvation, and expressed firm ideas concerning the ideal shape of society. It also defended its convictions with evangelistic zeal. In the crush of Revolutionary events the struggle of liberty against oppression colored every aspect of life. Where classic Puritanism had defined its comprehensive vision of life in terms of the battle against sin and the struggle for righteousness, Revolutionary Christianity tended to visualize oppression as the greatest enemy and liberty as the highest good. This shift from comprehensive religious categories to religio-political ones did not, moreover, spring *de novo* from Lexington Green. As far back as the early years of the French and Indian War, colonists had begun to link sin with oppression, righteousness with liberty. Solomon Williams, for example, told soldiers going out to that conflict that they were fighting "for all that is worth Valuing in the World." He left no doubts concerning what the soldiers were being sent out to accomplish:

> To Recover, to Secure our just Rights, to Save our Properties, to Preserve our Estates, to Secure the Rights and Liberties of Serving God, the Freedom of the Churches of Christ in this land, the Freedom

of the Gospel, and the Pure Religion of it, to preserve
your Selves, and your country from Slavery, to Secure
the Welfare of all our Posterity, the Liberty, and
Honour of our Nation.[11]

By 1776 Great Britain had replaced France as the
object of dread, but nothing had taken the place of liberty
as the cornerstone of the colonial scale of values. Abraham
Keteltas, a Presbyterian minister, preached a sermon on
October 5, 1777, in Newburyport, Massachusetts, in which
he argued that "the most precious remains of civil liberty
the world can now boast of, are lodged in our hands." Since
this was so, the War for Independence itself became

the cause of truth, against error and falsehood, . . . the
cause of pure and undefiled religion, against bigotry,
superstition, and human inventions. . . . In short, it
is the cause of heaven against hell — of the kind Parent
of the universe against the prince of darkness, and
the destroyer of the human race.[12]

Another Presbyterian, Nathaniel Whitaker of Salem, Massachusetts, contributed his mite to the Patriot cause by analyzing the roots of American Loyalism in two strongly worded
works: *Antitode Against Toryism* and *The Reward of Toryism*. From Whitaker's point of view, anyone who supported
the corrupt Parliament could only be a captive of venality
and a servant of tyranny. Such a one was, in the words of
a historian of the Presbyterian role in the war, "convicted
of treason (placing private interest above public good) and
impiety (putting self before God)."[13] Patriotic Christians did
not lose their deep convictions about sin and righteousness,
but during the war they tended increasingly to redirect these
convictions in order to further religiously the very truths
which Whigs propounded in the political sphere.

11. Solomon Williams, *The Duty of Christian Soldiers* . . . (New London: T. & J. Green, 1755), pp. 26, 25.
12. Abraham Keteltas, *God arising and pleading his People's Cause; or,
the American War in favor of Liberty, against the Measures and arms
of Great Britain, shewn to be the Cause of God* . . . (Newbury-Port:
John Mycall for Edmund Sawyer, 1777), pp. 27, 30.
13. "Muskets in the Pulpit: Part II," *Journal of the Presbyterian Historical Society,* XXXII (March, 1954), 39.

Throughout the Revolution, ministers did continue to call individuals to repentance and belief in God. The Connecticut General Association of 1776, whose analysis of the conflict was mentioned in the Preface, also called for "sincere Repentance, and a thoro' Reformation."[14] Even Charles Chauncy, who as an opponent of the evangelistic strain of New England religion did not often go in for this type of appeal, denounced Americans in 1778 for having "dishonored Christ, neglected his salvation, abused his grace, and grieved his spirit."[15] Yet even here in the most strictly religious part of life — the relationship of a soul to God — Christian republicanism injected a political note. Although ministers had referred to military victories as God's "salvation" as far back as the French and Indian War,[16] this emphasis took on new meaning during the Revolution. After the Port of Boston had been closed by the Intolerable Acts, the pastors of Connecticut wrote words of comfort to their Boston colleagues. In particular, they prayed that in the present distress God would "ensure Salvation to us."[17] The use of the language of redemption in a political context wavered between mere metaphor, as when the Congregationalist Ebenezer Cleaveland likened Christian salvation to the conversion of a crown officer into a Son of Liberty, and outright identification, as when the Presbyterian Robert Smith in 1781 spoke of "the cause of America [as] the cause of Christ."[18] Although such an identification is striking, it

---

14. *The Records of the General Association of Ye Colony of Connecticut*, pp. 89-90.

15. Charles Chauncy, *The Accursed Thing must be taken away from among a People* ... (Boston: Thomas & John Fleet, 1778), p. 13.

16. See George Beckwith, *That People A Safe, and happy People, who have God for, and among them* ... (New London: T. Green, 1756), p. 25.

17. In William C. Fowler, "The Ministers of Connecticut in the Revolution," *Centennial Papers, Published by Order of the Congregational Churches of Connecticut* (Hartford: Case, Lockwood & Brainard, 1877), p. 35.

18. Ebenezer Cleaveland, *The abounding Grace of God toward notorious Sinners* ... (Salem: S. & E. Hall, 1776); Robert Smith, *The Obligations of the Confederate States of North America to Praise God ... for the various interpositions of his providence in their favour, during their contests with Great Britain* ... (Philadelphia: Francis Bailey, 1782), p. 33.

is not surprising in light of the amalgamation of Whig and Christian points of view, and particularly in light of the fervent millennial aura surrounding Patriotic aspirations. In a very real sense, Christian republicans were able to view the Patriotic cause as the banner of salvation and the progress of America as the outworking of the plan of redemption.

Whig Christianity did not necessarily seek to open the floodgates of freedom at home as it plumped for liberty from Great Britain. Whigs believed that only in a society where contending social groupings and special interests were in balance could corruption be curtailed. When any part of society gained inordinate power, be it the king, Parliament, or the popular masses, corruption followed inevitably. To preserve freedom, therefore, it was necessary that the talk of liberty directed against Great Britain not be applied indiscriminately in America. The Federalists of the 1790's with their cautious concern for balanced government and wary suspicion of the democratic mob only highlighted aspects of American thought that had been prominent even before the Revolution. From the religious side, ardent contention for liberty against Great Britain was often matched by cautious restraints on the exercise of domestic freedom. Jonathan Mayhew, who spoke out so forthrightly in asserting the right to overthrow unjust rulers, who challenged attempts by the Church of England to gain strength in the colonies, and who fervently demanded the repeal of the Stamp Act as an illegal infringement upon colonial liberty, exerted considerable effort in dampening antinomian fires after the repeal of the Act. His famous sermon heralding a normalization of colonial-British relations after the repeal called on Americans to resume their wonted stations in life and to forsake the excesses that had attended agitation over the Stamp Act:

> Let us all apply ourselves with diligence, and in the fear of God, to the duties of our respective stations.... Even the poor, and labouring part of the community, whom I am very far from despising, have had so much to say about government and politics, in the late times of danger, tumult and confusion, that

> many of them seemed to forget, they had any thing
> to *do*. Methinks it would now be expedient for *them,*
> and perhaps most of us, to do something more, and
> talk something less, . . . letting things return peaceably
> into their old channels, and natural courses, after so
> long an interruption.[19]

However much they exhorted their congregations to extreme views against Great Britain, clergymen usually counseled moderation on the home front. Christian Whigs did not want to replace the oppression of a corrupt British aristocracy with the tyranny of a dissolute native anarchy.

If the synthesis of Whig and Christian points of view sought to restrain upheaval at home, it placed few restraints on its Patriotic rhetoric. Since the Great Awakening, the colonists had grown accustomed to an emotive style of discourse directed more at emotions and the will than at reason and the mind. This type of rhetoric continued without abatement during the Revolutionary period even as more strictly religious matters gave way before the amalgam of religion and politics which we have called Whig Christianity. Jonathan Mayhew, who had himself renounced the particular theology of the Awakening, displayed a rhetorical style that was as "evangelistic" in the service of liberty as Whitefield's was in the service of the gospel. In the very same sermon in which Mayhew counseled restraint for the masses, his own emotions carried him into a long and rapturous peroration on the theme of liberty. The "charms" of liberty, Mayhew declared, "have daily captured me more and more." Liberty was a "celestial Maid, the daughter of God, and, excepting his Son, the firstborn of heaven"; in heaven it would be eternal bliss "to enjoy forever the 'glorious liberty of the sons of God.'"[20] During the Stamp crisis itself, opponents of the Act heartened each other by calling those who shared their opinions the "Lord's anointed" and the "darlings of Providence."[21]

---

19. Jonathan Mayhew, *The Snare Broken* . . . (Boston: Draper, Gill, and Fleet, 1776), pp. 41-42.

20. *Ibid.*, pp. 34, 36, 37.

21. See Oscar Zeichner, *Connecticut's Years of Controversy, 1750-1776* (Chapel Hill: University of North Carolina Press, 1949), pp. 51, 74.

As the actual conflict with Great Britain drew near, pulpits throughout the land rang with fervent appeals that mixed Christianity and Patriotism in equal measure. In 1774, Samuel Sherwood of Weston, Connecticut, preached a sermon of "Scriptural Injunctions to Civil Rulers" in which the conflict between Britain and the colonies was described as between "the true friends to the rights of humanity, — our dear country, and constitutional liberties and privileges, civil and religious: And the base, traitorous and perfidious enemies thereto."[22] In 1776, Samuel West addressed the Massachusetts Assembly in the annual election sermon with even more fervent rhetoric. In the face of the "wanton exertion of arbitrary power" and a "barbarity unknown to Turks and Mahometan infidels," he asked his hearers, "Does it not then highly concern us all to stand fast in the liberty wherewith heaven has made us free, and to strive to get the victory over the beast and his image, over every species of tyranny?"[23] During the conflict itself, Patriotic ministers encouraged their people with the assurance that "liberty is given us by God" and that "we have such a good and righteous God to look to: a God who governs the world and disposes the nations. We will go on to complete that freedom which we have begun to contend for."[24] The intensity with which many Christians embraced Whig thought and with which Christian libertarianism was proclaimed was a consistent reflection of the thorough merger of Christian and Whig ideologists. The new synthesis of Christian Whiggery exerted as penetrating an influence on American Patriots as the older Puritan synthesis had on the residents of seventeenth-century New England. It was a potent force in support of a free United States.

22. Samuel Sherwood, *A Sermon, Containing Scriptural Injunctions to Civil Rulers, and all Free-born Subjects . . .* (New Haven: T. & S. Green, 1774), p. ix.
23. Samuel West, *A Sermon Preached before the Honorable Council and the honorable House of Representatives, of the Colony of the Massachusetts-Bay . . .* (Boston: John Gill, 1776), pp. 53, 67.
24. Jacob Green, *Documents Relating to the Revolutionary History of the State of New Jersey,* ed. William Nelson, Vol. IV (Trenton: State Gazette Publishing Co., 1914), 344, 346.

In order to have a better picture of Christian Patriotism during the Revolution, it would be helpful to look more closely at specific individuals. Brief sketches of the thoughts and actions of two American clergymen, one an influential college president, the other a relatively obscure parish minister, can help us to see more clearly the nature of the bond between Patriotism and Christianity. John Witherspoon (1723-1794) had been reluctant to accept the presidency of Princeton College when called to this post by Presbyterians in America, but almost as soon as he arrived from Scotland in 1768, his forceful personality and popular teaching made him a leader in both political and religious affairs. Upon arriving to take up his duties at Princeton, Witherspoon joined what Leonard Trinterud called "the radical independence party in New Jersey."[25] So rapidly did he rise to prominence in colonial political affairs that even some of his fellow Presbyterians were skeptical of his mixing "Civil and Ecclesiastical Power." If we complain about the Church of England making no distinction between politics and religion, they criticized, how can we defend actions by our own clergymen like Witherspoon when they run for office and exercise direct political power? Once hostilities actually broke out with Great Britain, criticism from the Presbyterian ranks receded only to be replaced by rebukes from the other side. One crown official in the colonies wrote back to England that the labors of such clergymen as Witherspoon so influenced the shape of the conflict that it had become "at the Bottom very much a religious War."[26]

Witherspoon's labors as president of Princeton were perhaps as important for the Patriot cause as his public office-holding and his public defense of Whiggery. One historian of colonial Presbyterianism has written that the British should have called Princeton "Witherspoon's seminary of sedition" in light of its Revolutionary influence on a generation of American ministers and public servants.[27] James Madison was the most well known of the many prominent

25. *A Re-examination of Colonial Presbyterianism*, p. 243.
26. In "Muskets in the Pulpit: Part I," p. 229.
27. "Muskets in the Pulpit: Part II," p. 42.

leaders of the early United States who learned statecraft as well as theology from Witherspoon.

In his theology Witherspoon was a traditional and orthodox conservative. He did not, however, possess the revivalistic zeal or the dogmatic rigor of the Edwardsean New Divinity. Although he shared Edwards' commitment to a high view of God's authority, he was inclined to lay greater weight on the natural, as opposed to the revealed, law of God. In this particular he manifested his indebtedness to the Scottish version of Enlightenment thought. When Witherspoon migrated to America, he carried with him the precepts of Scottish Realism, the dominant philosophical position in eighteenth-century Scottish universities. The emphases which this school placed on man as a free agent, on the self-evident nature of moral intuition, and on the importance of the social contract for relations within society set Witherspoon's thought apart from any of the recognizable theological parties in America. While he shared all of the orthodoxy, much of the piety, and some of the evangelistic intensity of the Presbyterian New Side revivalists, he also partook of the reliance on reason and the dependence on the social covenant characteristic of the Old Side anti-revivalists.

Although Witherspoon is difficult to classify theologically, his political beliefs placed him squarely among the Patriotic Whigs. His theological commitment to the importance of natural law blended nicely with the Whig emphasis on natural rights. Believing that in the social contract men gave up some natural rights in order to preserve essential freedoms, Witherspoon saw British actions as a threat to the liberties which had been granted by nature and guaranteed by the social compact. The importance of the covenant in Witherspoon's thought predisposed him to see a sanctifying force in arguments from natural law. It also enabled him to castigate British violations of colonial charters on religious grounds. Religious thinking came more directly into the open in considering the concept of "dominion." To Witherspoon, as to most Presbyterians, final dominion on earth was God's alone. Dominion among men was to be exercised only by mutual consent. In order to insure that no human agency would arrogate for itself powers belonging to God alone, Witherspoon considered a mixed government in which dominion was shared as the best human form. British attempts to exercise authority "in all cases whatsoever" flew in the face not only of the best human principles of government but also of God's rightful place as the Lord of the world.

As the Revolutionary crisis developed, Witherspoon's activities on behalf of the Patriot cause reflected the thorough mixture of Whig and Christian elements in his thinking. On May 20, 1775, a synodical letter drafted by Witherspoon and sent to the Presbyterian churches in the influential Synod of New York and Philadelphia endorsed the political viewpoint of the American Whigs. It called on the people to remember that the House of Hanover itself, of which George III was then the representative, had come to the throne when Englishmen overthrew the corrupt and impious James II. One year later in a fast-day sermon of May 17, Witherspoon took the unprecedented step of openly discussing politics in the pulpit. Never before had a Presbyterian of such stature used the pulpit so openly to propagate such a partisan point of view. The printed edition of this sermon also contained an address to Witherspoon's fellow Scots in America. In it he argued that since Britain demanded unconditional colonial submission, the defense of colonial freedom could not be separated from a defense of colonial independence.

Witherspoon was elected as a delegate from New Jersey to the Continental Congress where he became the only clergyman to affix his signature to the Declaration of Independence. He served for approximately five years in the Continental Congress, and although the exact nature of his contributions to its deliberations is not known, his service on over 120 congressional committees suggests the extent of his energy and influence.

The way in which libertarianism and Christianity mingled in Witherspoon's thinking is seen in two works produced in 1783 after the successful termination of the war. From the Whig side, a synodical letter expressed gratitude for "the general and almost universal attachment of the Presby-

terian body to the cause of liberty and the rights of mankind."[28] From the Christian side, Witherspoon preached a
sermon on the national day of Thanksgiving, December 11,
1783, in which he analyzed what had recently taken place:

> The separation of this country from Britain
> has been of God; for every step the British took to
> prevent seemed to accelerate it, which has generally
> been the case when men have undertaken to go in op-
> position to the course of Providence, and to make war
> with the nature of things.[29]

Moses Mather (1719-1806), a Congregational minister in Darien, Connecticut, was far less well known and
much less influential in the course of Revolutionary events
than President Witherspoon. Yet in his humble life the subtle
but deep interpenetration of Whig and Christian ideas is
illustrated as strikingly as in Witherspoon's prestigious career.
Mather was active as a pastor, a theologian, and a Patriot
throughout the latter half of the eighteenth century when
old religious and political convictions were beginning to give
way to newer beliefs. His theological labors were directed
largely toward a modification of traditional orthodoxy and
a resistance to the Edwardsean desire to preserve the church
for just those who gave specific evidence of their regeneration. He took a deep interest in the political fate of the country, supporting colonial claims against Parliament in his
rousing tract of 1775, *America's Appeal to the Impartial
World*. His Connecticut election sermon for 1781 described
in considerable detail the high place of America in God's
esteem. Mather's ardent Patriotism received a backhanded
compliment from the Tories of New York and southwestern
Connecticut, who twice captured him and subjected him to
difficult months in a New York City prison.

The direction of Mather's theology was revealed
most clearly in a controversy over standards for church membership with a disciple of Jonathan Edwards, Joseph Bellamy.
Mather argued that all who wished to be associated with

---

28. *Ibid.,* p. 51.
29. *Ibid.,* p. 48.

a church and who were free of public scandal should be allowed to become members. Bellamy, on the other hand, held that only those who by profession and practice gave evidence that God had truly saved them were to be granted admission. In the course of this debate Mather redefined several parts of traditional Calvinism, particularly in order to accommodate more modern concepts of reason and nature. It was, for example, "very obvious to reason" that people even while still unconverted could properly use the church as a means of grace since men have "clear and distinct ideas" about what regeneration actually entails.[30] The strict church covenant defended by Joseph Bellamy was in error since God had graciously taken into covenant all in a society who wished to be part of a church, even if many were conscious of not yet being truly Christians. Mather by no means rejected the theology of Bellamy's tradition, but he did redirect it in line with more modern canons of reasonableness.

These canons also guided the exposition of his political thought. Mather's *America's Appeal* argued that the "English government was constituted upon the foundation of reason; and the natural rights of subjects." Hence, when Parliament illegally struck at the colonists' rights and privileges, this was not merely a tyrannous assault but a violation of the principles underlying the British government itself. By thus breaking the solemn agreements guaranteed by colonial charters, Parliament forfeited its rights to colonial obedience. The religious background to Mather's thinking on contractual relations was revealed when he referred to the colonial charters as "sacred compacts."[31] On the domestic ecclesiastical scene, Mather had expanded his concept of the covenant to include all but the openly scandalous members of New England society. In his political works he saw Parliament's violation of the covenants between Great Britain and her colonies as the most compelling justification for independence. The seriousness with which Mather argued about church covenants was reflected in his

---

30. Moses Mather, *A Systematic View of Divinity . . .* (Stamford: Nathan Weed [written ca. 1775, published 1813]), pp. 181, 60.
31. *America's Appeal,* pp. 8, 59.

religiously colored castigation of Britain for breaking its covenanted word with the colonies.

Mather's religious perception of the struggle for independence came across with greater clarity in his Connecticut election sermon of 1781. He marveled that "our affections are weaned from Great-Britain, by similar means and almost as miraculously as the Israelites from Egypt." He maintained that "the over-ruling hand of divine providence has been often so conspicuous in the events of the present war, as to extort a confession, even from infidelity itself, that it is God that fighteth for us." And he could urge Connecticut's elected officials to fulfill their tasks with the knowledge that God "hath loved this State."[32] While Mather's ideas were not as influential as Witherspoon's in shaping colonial resistance to Britain, they were indicative of how thoroughly the religious point of view shared the perspective of the Whig arguments. Witherspoon, Mather, and many other believers in the colonies could merge Whiggery and Christianity so effortlessly since both seemed to be grounded in the character and laws of God and to point in only one direction where the conflict with Great Britain was concerned.

One of the ways in which Moses Mather's Christian Patriotism expressed itself was by comparing the colonies to God's ancient people, Israel. Indeed, it often appears that colonial ministers felt the history of Israel was merely a foreshadowing of the fully realized glories of an American Christian nation. As far back as the French and Indian War, ministers had begun to conceive of the British empire, and more specifically the American colonies, as God's unique people. In a sermon preached to commemorate Wolfe's victory at Quebec in 1759, Solomon Williams asked his listeners to consider "how our Relations to God resemble those of the Israelites . . . how our Obligations and Engagements are similar." As Williams described the war with France, the grand realities of Israel's history and of the whole history

---

32. Moses Mather, *Sermon, Preached in the Audience of the General Assembly of the State of Connecticut* . . . (New London: Timothy Green, 1781), pp. 62, 16, 18.

of redemption were assimilated into the equally compelling realities of New England's history:

> He has been our Strength, and is become our Salvation. After our Hands have been three Years in a Sort tied up, God has in the course of these last triumphed gloriously. Pharaoh's Chariots, and his Host hath he cast into the Sea, his chosen Captains also are drowned in the Red Sea of Blood.[33]

Closer to the war itself, an anonymous layman argued:

> That the English nation, as such having universally received the Christian religion and established it as a natural religion ... and having formed all their laws and regulations of civil society, agreeable to its holy precepts, have a right to look upon themselves as much in visible covenant with God as ever the Jews had.[34]

Once it became apparent that Great Britain's corruption excluded it from the special blessings of God to "his people," the identification of the colonies as God's chosen people became even more pronounced.

Charles Chauncy of Boston illustrated the moving power of identifying Israel and the colonies in several of his works. According to Chauncy, as the Jews had been delivered from Egypt and, later, from the destruction threatened by Ahasuerus, so had New England been delivered from the Stamp Act. The founding fathers of New England had been saved from tyranny in England and established in a new land just as God had saved his people from Egypt and established them in Canaan. In short, Chauncy could assure the Americans in 1770, "Perhaps, there are no people, now dwelling on the face of the earth, who may, with greater pertinency, adopt the language of king *David,* and say, 'our fathers trusted in thee; they trusted, and thou didst deliver

---

33. Solomon Williams, *The Relations of God's People to him ...* (New London: Timothy Green, 1760), pp. 14-15, 19.
34. Anonymous, *The Parishioner, Having Studied the Point ...* (Hartford: Green & Watson, 1769), p. 22.

them.' " In that same discourse Chauncy brought together his concept of divine providence, his Whig convictions, and his identification of the colonies with Israel by paraphrasing Psalm 122 as a review of the election sermon in colonial Massachusetts:

> We were wont to take to ourselves words, and say 'we were glad when they said unto us, let us go into the house of the Lord. Our feet shall stand within thy gates, O BOSTON, BOSTON is a city compact together, whither the tribes, throughout the province, by their representatives, the tribes of the Lord, assemble to give thanks to the name of the Lord,' preparatory to the exercise of one of our important CHARTER-RIGHTS, the ELECTION of his MAJESTY'S COUNCIL.[35]

Many more examples could be given of this same confident assumption that the history of Israel was being reenacted in colonial America. To cite merely one illustration by a non-Congregationalist from some place other than New England, George Duffield, a Presbyterian from Philadelphia, preached a sermon on August 10, 1777, in which Britain was likened to Babylon and to Egypt while America was described as Judah.[36] The end result of this identification of Israel and the colonies was that the war against Britain could be fought for country and for God at one and the same time. The relative character of the conflict, or doubts about its rectitude or necessity, could be set aside if it were perceived as an ultimate struggle between the people of God and the hosts of darkness.

In a more practical area, the deep interconnections between libertarianism and Christianity were also seen in fear of the Church of England. The coalescence of Whig and Christian viewpoints meant that differences with the Church

35. Charles Chauncy, *A Discourse on "the good News from a far Country"*... (1766), in *The Pulpit of the American Revolution,* ed. Thornton, pp. 129, 137; *Trust in God, the Duty of a People in a Day of Trouble*... (Boston: Daniel Kneeland for Thomas Leverett, 1770), pp. 13, 21; p. 6; p. 32.
36. See "Muskets in the Pulpit: Part I," p. 243.

of England were viewed in political as well as religious terms. The end result was that fear of the Church of England, particularly of the establishment of a bishop in the colonies, became a major constituent of the political estrangement from Great Britain. At the height of the Stamp Act controversy, John Adams had published his *Dissertation on the Canon and Feudal Law*. Adams, who enjoyed listening to the Rev. George Duffield's Patriotic sermons when he was in Philadelphia, outlined in theory what other Whigs had begun to put in practice — that arbitrary government in the church was part of the general assault on liberty. During 1759 and 1760, Patrick Henry of Virginia had argued in court against Anglican claims to stated ecclesiastical revenues. In this celebrated "Two-Penny" Case, Henry maintained that the king could not arbitrarily set aside acts of the Virginia legislature dealing with the Anglican church. Henry also contended that the ecclesiastical authority of the Church of England needed to be curbed by the same checks and balances applicable to other institutions in society. Four years later Jonathan Mayhew published a scathing denunciation of the actions and ideas of an Anglican "missionary" to Boston, the Rev. East Apthorp. Mayhew denounced in biting language Apthorp's claim that only the Church of England was truly orthodox or truly worthy of universal public support.

Objections which colonists raised against the Church of England paralleled objections against Parliament and the entire administration of the British system. The Anglican hierarchy was marked by corruption and venality; it exercised a dangerously unrestricted power in the choice of bishops and the establishment of ecclesiastical regulations; and it encouraged the most despotic and absolutistic features of the British system.

Ezra Stiles, a minister in Newport, Rhode Island, before assuming the presidency of Yale College, provides a good illustration of the way in which anti-Anglican thought entered the political arena during the Revolutionary period. Stiles' commitment to the Real Whig idea of freedom and his belief in free rational inquiry became the principal factors contributing to his intense fear of the Church of England. In his *Discourse on the Christian Union* (1761) Stiles proposed an intercolonial fellowship of Calvinistic churches, a fellowship which would have at least one eye cocked for the encroaching threat of Anglicanism. As the overt tensions leading to the break with Great Britain emerged, Stiles saw the Church of England with an increasingly jaundiced eye. His suspicions against the Anglicans had been aroused when as a young Yale graduate he had been solicited for an Anglican pulpit through purely mercenary and social inducements. Over the years, as could be expected from one who perceived the world through Whig spectacles, he came to see an increased menace to civil and religious liberty from the grasping, corrupt, and authoritarian Church of England. His own reading of history supported the view that religious and civil tyranny went hand in hand. Moreover, he thought he could see an Anglican lust for power everywhere in the colonies: the Church of England demanded public support for religious establishments in the South, it had taken over the board of trustees of the Redwood Library in Newport, it had tried to take over the College of New Jersey, it regularly connived with the Free Masons, it stirred up Old Light-New Light differences in Connecticut, it proselytized through bribes instead of reasonable argument, it had tried to have Rhode Island's precious charter revoked, it had stirred up trouble at the time of the Stamp Act, and it had facilitated the movement of British troops into Boston during 1770. If the Church of England's grasping attempts to monopolize ecclesiastical power were not checked, Stiles and many others thought the attempts would lead directly to similar assaults on civil freedom as well.

It would be incorrect to think that all American Christians, and particularly all descendants of the Puritans, supported the Patriot cause with the same vigor or in the same frame of reference. Our next chapter looks at several Calvinists who, however Patriotic, questioned certain aspects of the common Christian Whig point of view. Some Christian Patriots continued to urge repentance and belief while discussing the evils of British tyranny. In most cases, however, even these urgings partook of the conflated Whig-Christian stance. Calls for repentance and reform did not always hold out the prospect of favor with God through Christ as much as they asserted that God would bless the war effort if Americans behaved themselves. When Moses Mather, for example, spoke of the sins of the colonists, he referred more to the "divine judgments" such as "abominations" pull down upon a people than to God's fundamental displeasure with them.[37] So pervasive was the Whig-Christian ideology that not even the most strictly spiritual areas remained outside of its influence.

Shades of difference corresponding to theological points of view did exist to some degree, but these should not be stressed inordinately. It is true that some New Light followers of Jonathan Edwards, particularly those who were concerned about the purity of the church, did distinguish between the cause of America and the cause of Christ. Unlike many of his fellow ministers, the New Light Joseph Bellamy did not talk of military victory over Great Britain as "salvation." In one letter to his son who was serving in Washington's army he revealed the true priority of his values: "My desire and prayer to God is, that my son Jonathan may be saved. And then whatever happens to America or to you, this year or next, you will be happy forever."[38] The contrast of Bellamy's statement to the words of the Old Light Moses Mather, when Mather received the body of his son who had died while a British prisoner of war, suggests the different attitude of some Old and New Lights to the war: "I had rather see him a corpse, than to have him join the enemies of his country."[39] Old Lights in general tended to display a greater concern for social stability than did New Lights, as in Charles Chauncy's sermon of 1778 in which "The Accursed Thing" besetting the colonies turns out to be not a particular rejection of God but the wartime infla-

37. *Sermon to the Connecticut Assembly,* p. 22.
38. Joseph Bellamy, *The Works of Joseph Bellamy* (Boston: Doctrinal Tract & Book Society, 1850), Vol. I, xl.
39. William B. Sprague, *Annals of the American Pulpit* (New York: Robert Carter & Brothers, 1857-1869), Vol. I, 427.

tion that was playing havoc with clerical stipends. In spite of these tendencies, nevertheless, both New Lights and Old Lights accepted the basic synthesis of Whig and Christian ideas. Individuals from all theological camps actively pursued the goal of a Christian republic.

Finally, the extent to which Patriotic convictions entered into ecclesiastical considerations is a last testimony to the marriage of libertarian and Christian sentiments. So important had Whig verities become to many Christians that it seemed deviant for anyone to profess to be a Christian without also supporting colonial Patriotism. "An Address to the Ministers of the Presbyterian congregations in North Carolina" from the Synod of New York and Philadelphia illustrates this type of thinking. Written just on the eve of the war itself, this Address urged North Carolina ministers to unite, trust God, support nonimportation of British goods, and back the Continental Congress. If the North Carolina Presbyterians could not do these things, the Address went on, "we can have no fellowship with you; our soul shall weep for you in secret, but will not be able any longer to number you among our friends, nor the friends of liberty."[40] The Presbyterian Synod of New England declared in September, 1776, that anyone "suspected to be inimical to the liberties of the independent States of America" should be denied "a seat in this judicature."[41] Suiting the action to the word, this synod ejected one minister who supported the British and suspended another until he could give convincing proof of his Patriotism. While these incidents may appear extreme, they were not far from the normal behavior of those Christians who had seasoned their Christianity with libertarianism.

The confluence of Whig ideology and Christian conviction, particularly by the heirs of the Reformed traditions, exerted a great influence on the perception of the conflict. The notion that God had singularly blessed and would uniquely guide the American colonies was an idea

40. In "Presbyterians Approach the American Revolution: Part II," p. 171.
41. In "Muskets in the Pulpit: Part II," p. 41.

whose ramifications have continued to influence the course of American religious history to the present day. Yet so clearly did Christian truths seem to be in agreement with the Whig world view that very few Patriotic Christians were able to analyze objectively the bond between their religious and political beliefs. American Christians persuaded of the reality of this connection saw the War for Independence religiously and their religion Patriotically. With the Connecticut election preacher of 1777, they were ready to ascribe the highest religious value to the conflict with Great Britain and to envision the rosiest prospects for America's future:

> Lo! the angel Gabriel comes.
> From him that sits upon the throne;
> All nations hear the great Jehovah's will;
> America, henceforth separate,
> Sit as Queen among the nations.

* * * *

> Live, Live, Live
> Beloved of the Lord, until he comes.
> Whose right it is to reign:
> Call her Free and Independent STATES of AMERICA!
> Hallelujah, Praise the Lord. Amen.[42]

42. John Devotion, *The Duty and Interest of a People to sanctify the Lord of Hosts . . .* (Hartford: Eben. Watson, 1777), p. 39.

IV   *The Reforming Response*

> *Christian Patriots did not entirely neglect more*
strictly religious matters during the Revolutionary period.
As Leonard Trinterud put it in his history of colonial Presbyterianism: "Seldom . . . did the preacher forget to sound
an authentic Christian note of the Gospel, its call for repentance, renewal, and godly living."[1] Even granting the truth
of Trinterud's observation, however, the modern reader of
sermons from the Revolutionary era receives the impression
that such spiritual matters were present more as a sop to
Puritan traditions than as a central part of the preacher's
message. Though Moses Mather roundly denounced "vice and
immorality" in his Connecticut election sermon of 1781,[2]
he exerted much more energy in recounting the divine blessings poured out upon the independent colonies. The colonists'
own evils, though frequently mentioned, were usually treated
with little of the intensity that went into the description
of British assaults on colonial liberty. However troubling
indigenous sins might be, they could not compare with the
utterly depraved actions of the British and their traitorous
American allies.

Some of the heirs of the Puritans, however, had
a different perspective on the Revolutionary conflict and
its spiritual implications for Americans. While subscribing

---

1. Leonard J. Tinterud, *The Forming of an American Tradition: A
Re-examination of Colonial Presbyterianism*, p. 154.
2. Moses Mather, *Sermon, Preached in the Audience of the General
Assembly of the State of Connecticut . . .*, p. 21.

in the main to the basic Whig precepts, these Christians held to a value higher than political libertarianism. As a consequence, such individuals were able to mount a stingingly specific campaign for repentance and reform within American society itself. They did not allow their awareness of British evil to crowd out diligent attention to colonial wrongs. Although these individuals were not nearly as common as the advocates of undifferentiated Christian republicanism, they were numerous enough to constitute a significant alternative to the way in which the Patriotic descendants of the Puritans approached the American Revolution. Members of other religious traditions also criticized aspects of colonial society from a religious perspective during the Revolution, and some of their criticisms will be noted in subsequent chapters. The importance of the individuals examined in this chapter rests in the fact that while they affirmed the Puritan heritage and adopted Whig convictions, they were nevertheless able to apply searching Christian criticism to the very movement which their fellow religionists supported with so little reservation.

An examination of the religious and theological backgrounds of these individuals provides some help in accounting for their ability to maintain the distinction between Christian and national values. It is noteworthy that they were mostly New Lights whose religious convictions were as intense as the political beliefs of the Whigs and whose theology was as carefully developed as the arguments of the libertarians. Because their specifically religious convictions were not swallowed up by political concerns, these rare Christians were able to maintain a capacity for judging good and evil beyond the perception of what was good or bad for the colonies. Besides calling urgently for general repentance, spiritual rebirth, and the renewal of society, they also urged specific reforms particularly in two areas: the establishment of religion and the practice of slaveholding.

Isaac Backus was only one of a large number of colonial Baptists who saw serious internal inconsistencies in the American struggle against British tyranny. Backus, like most colonial Baptists, was a product of the Great

Awakening. While working in the fields on August 22, 1741, he had, as he described it, been "enabled by divine light to see the perfect righteousness of Christ and the freeness and riches of His grace.... My heavy burden was gone, tormenting fears were fled, and my joy was unspeakable."[3] Because of his Baptist convictions, however, Backus was cut off from the established Congregational Church in New England, even from that group which included such leading revivalists as Edwards himself. The combination of religious commitments stemming from the Great Awakening and social-ecclesiastical viewpoints at variance with the colonial ecclesiastical mainstream combined to give Backus, and the Baptists in general, a singular perspective on the American Revolution. Baptists would later come to play an important role in shaping the American civil religion of the nineteenth and twentieth centuries, but during the Revolutionary age they stood for principles which set them apart from the many who readily joined Christianity and American nationalism.

Backus himself was heavily indebted to Jonathan Edwards in the construction of his theology. With Edwards he rejected human "means" as in any sense contributory to salvation; he held that conversion was accomplished by a palpable manifestation of grace; he was committed to the teachings of Scripture understood in a Reformed sense; and he argued that the church must reflect the purity of its Head. So close did Backus consider his own position to Edwards that some time after the Great Awakening he could write of "our Edwards."[4] Only in rejecting infant baptism did Backus deviate significantly from Edwards, and in Backus' opinion this rejection merely carried Edwards' own teaching to its logical conclusion by demanding clear signs of regeneration before allowing a person to be baptized and to enter the church.

---

3. In William G. McLoughlin, ed., *Isaac Backus on Church, State, and Calvinism* (Cambridge: Harvard University Press, 1968), pp. 2-3.
4. In Alan Heimert, *Religion and the American Mind From the Great Awakening to the Revolution* (Cambridge: Harvard University Press, 1966), p. 6.

The logic of the Great Awakening as it came to expression in Backus and the Baptists led to a particular concept of the relationship between God's true people (the church) and society at large. To the Baptists, the radically personal nature of saving grace and the subsequent necessity for a pure church brought the communal ideal undergirding New England's established church into question. While Backus was not so far ahead of his time as to abandon the vision of a Christian nation, he did call for an end to the governmental and legal apparatus which supported most of the churches in New England. To establish the Christian religion by legislation totally disregarded a cardinal gospel principle: it is not man's effort but God's grace which frees a man from sin and produces good works in his life. Since the gospel was necessarily personal and experiential, the ministrations of the state in religious affairs could only impede the free workings of grace and the gracious works of one whom God had set free. Like Roger Williams, whom he quoted, Backus thought that an established religion was only good for making hypocrites and for limiting God's freely given love by artificial human devices. Freedom from political oppression in general was a necessity if the gospel were to operate as it should. Restrictions imposed by religious establishments and the forced support of non-biblical practices bore the taint of tyranny whether in England or the colonies.

Backus set out the principles dividing the civil and religious spheres in his tract, *An Appeal to the Public for Religious Liberty against the Oppression of the Present Day* (1773):

> God has appointed two kinds of government in the world which are distinct in their nature and ought never to be confounded together, one of which is called civil the other ecclesiastical government. . . . God has always claimed it as his sole prerogative to determine by his own laws what his worship shall be, who shall minister in it, and how they shall be supported, so it

is evident that this prerogative has been, and still is, encroached upon in our land.[5]

In this essay Backus quoted Galatians 5:1 ("our blessed Lord and only Redeemer has commanded us to *stand fast in the liberty wherewith he has made us free*") to an end far different than that to which Jonathan Mayhew turned a similar text. While both Backus and Mayhew saw liberty threatened by the heavy hand of governmental interference, Mayhew viewed freedom primarily as a human possession given to all men by natural right. Backus, on the other hand, saw it as a divine gift to the regenerate from a sovereign God. The threat to liberty perceived by Mayhew was an assault on humanity; to Backus it was an attack on the true children of God.

For Backus and the Baptists, therefore, the shackles of the religious establishment had to be thrown off for the sake of the gospel. A clear line divided the church and society. New Lights who did not follow out the logic of their own ideas and who continued to baptize infants violated that line by numbering those who were possibly unregenerate among the elect; the Massachusetts and Connecticut legislatures violated it by passing laws governing the internal life of the church.

It was not a casual matter to adopt these positions in the New England of the mid-eighteenth century. Although New England was far more hospitable to its dissenters than England was to hers, those who were not part of New England's established church were forced to live with what the Baptists considered debilitating spiritual anomalies. Through taxes for the construction of Congregational churches, Baptists were forced to support practices such as infant baptism which they considered repugnant to Scripture. Because of the legislatures' rigid requirements for clerical education and ordination, Baptists were forced against conscience to modify the law of Christ for the church according to the laws of men. Baptists also held that good deeds,

---

5. *An Appeal to the Public for Religious Liberty* (1773), in *Isaac Backus on Church, State, and Calvinism*, pp. 312, 317.

such as giving for the financial support of a minister, must flow voluntarily from a heart made good by the regenerating work of God and not from legal coercion. In particular, Baptists were disturbed when the long arm of the law reached down to pluck away the goods or to restrict the liberty of those who followed their consciences and refused to abide by the laws of the Standing Order.

Isaac Backus and the Baptists were thus faced with an ambiguous situation when fellow New Englanders began to take up pens against British tyranny. Baptists were not at first convinced that they wanted any part of colonial Patriotism. Viewing the situation in moral rather than political terms, they considered maintaining neutrality in the political struggle. The coming of actual hostilities forced the Baptists to make a difficult decision. As late as 1771 Massachusetts Baptists had received relief from the king in a dispute with the Massachusetts assembly. In that year, the property of Baptists in Ashfield, Massachusetts, had been confiscated when they refused to contribute to the construction of a Congregational meetinghouse. When this case was appealed to the king, judgment was rendered in favor of the Baptists and against the Massachusetts legislature.

When the Massachusetts assembly again extended the act requiring Baptists to make complicated application for exemption from ecclesiastical levies in 1774, the Baptists were faced with a dilemma: whether to appeal again to the king in defense of a religious principle (and consequently to incur the obloquy of a colony aroused against the crown) or meekly to sacrifice a dearly held conviction against state interference in religion. The Baptists did not have any illusions about the virtue of king and Parliament, but they did view Great Britain as an effective counterfoil to the inimical Massachusetts assembly. The way out of this dilemma appeared in 1774 when Parliament revoked the Massachusetts charter and imposed the Intolerable Acts. Baptists were now convinced that Parliament was even more perfidious than the Massachusetts assembly and that reliance on Parliament was like leaning upon a fragile reed. In addition, the Baptists now had a higher American judiciary, the

Continental Congress in Philadelphia, in which to argue their case against Massachusetts. In appealing to the Continental Congress instead of Parliament, they could also show where their loyalties lay in the political conflict. It was, however, only when the threat to civil, and hence religious, liberty seemed greater from the king and Parliament than from the colonial assemblies that most Baptists turned to the Patriot cause espoused by their Congregational neighbors.

Even though Baptists came to support independence in large numbers, they did not forget their fundamental religious commitments. Unlike many of the other heirs of the Puritans who failed to distinguish between the cause of Christ and the cause of the independent colonies, Baptists such as Isaac Backus saw that the Patriot cause also needed reform. Before the Baptists had committed themselves to the Patriotic effort, Backus pointed out in *A Seasonable Plea for Liberty of Conscience against Some Late Violent Oppressive Proceedings* (1770) that "many who are filling the nation with the cry of Liberty and against oppressors are at the same time themselves violating the dearest of all rights, LIBERTY OF CONSCIENCE."[6]

Backus's *Appeal for Religious Liberty* (1773) is a classic example of how certain religious convictions maintained their integrity in the face of the dominant libertarianism of the Revolutionary period. Using the very arguments which the Patriots directed against Great Britain, Backus levelled a severe rebuke against the ecclesiastical tyranny of New England. Rather than translating the gospel into Whig categories as so many other ministers did, Backus sought to enlist Whiggery for the cause of Christ. If the colonies were concerned about the threat to their property from Britain, what should Baptists think about the colonists themselves?

A very great grievance which our country has justly complained of is that by some late proceed-

---

6. In William G. McLoughlin, *Isaac Backus and the American Pietistic Tradition* (Boston: Little, Brown, 1967), p. 122.

ings [of Parliament] a man's house or locks cannot secure either his person or his property from oppressive officers. Pray then consider what our brethren have suffered at Ashfield?

Backus, further, thought that intense concern over taxation without representation should have a domestic as well as a foreign focus:

We agree with the committee of our honored legislature in saying there is an essential difference between persons being taxed *where they are represented* and being taxed where they are not so. Therefore the whole matter very much turns upon this point, viz., Whether our *civil* legislature are in truth our representation in *religious* affairs or not?

In another exploitation of the popular Whig rhetoric, Backus asked pointedly why artificial limits had been placed on the idea of slavery:

Now how often have we been told that he is not a freeman but a slave whose person and goods are not at his own but another's disposal? . . . But how is our world filled with such madness concerning spiritual tyrants! How far have pride and infidelity, covetousness and luxury, yea, deceit and cruelty, these foreigners which came from Hell, carried their influence, and spread their baneful mischiefs in our world! Yet who is willing to own that he has been deceived and enslaved by them?[7]

Those who equated the Patriot cause with all that was good and Christian were quick to see the ambiguity in the Baptists' stance as treason. When Backus went to plead the cause of the Baptists before the Continental Congress at Philadelphia in 1774, it was rumored that he intended to alienate the other colonies from New England. Ezra Stiles, in whose mind the causes of God's people and the American nation were closely joined, could not see the crucial distinc-

_____

7. *Appeal for Religious Liberty,* in *Isaac Backus on Church, State, and Calvinism,* pp. 340, 332, 311.

tion that was so fundamental to the Baptists' position — that religious aspects of colonial life could be criticized by someone who was not a Tory. In his diary for September 4, 1776, Stiles recorded his construction of the Baptists' actions:

> The Baptists of New England were for taking sides with the Ministry [Great Britain]. As appeared in their proposed Application to the Continental Congress in the fall of 1774, and their laboring to make it a Condition, of using their Interest in Rhode Island Assembly for levying Troops after the Hostilities of Lexington, that Massachusetts Assembly should abolish their persecuting Laws [that is, the establishment of Congregationalism by law].[8]

In spite of aspersions cast upon their Patriotism, Baptists served loyally with the continental forces and supported independence actively once the actual fighting had begun. Backus' own son served in the colonial army. It is evident, however, that the controlling ideas with which Backus and many Baptists approached the American Revolution were not those of the Christian Whigs. For the Baptists, "liberty of conscience" had very little to do with the fear of economic or political slavery. It had, on the other hand, very much to do with religious, moral, and spiritual freedom. The ideology which governed the participation of Isaac Backus and the Baptists in the Revolutionary era was one that could not be assimilated into the patterns of Whig Christianity. Even after they had become open Patriots, most Baptists continued to be concerned for spiritual affairs. Through their spokesman, Isaac Backus, they continued to distinguish religious from civil goals and to preserve the distinction between Patriotism and Christianity.

Those who made this distinction were not limited to the Baptists: Jonathan Parsons, a New Light Presbyterian minister in Newburyport, Massachusetts, denounced the Con-

---

8. *The Literary Diary of Ezra Stiles,* ed. Franklin Bowditch Dexter (New York: Charles Scribner's Sons, 1901), Vol. II, 51.

gregational establishment for complaining about British imperial tyranny while maintaining local ecclesiastical oppression. Nor was the criticism of religious establishments proceeding from recognition of the distinction between Patriotism and Christianity carried out on limited terms. Israel Holly, a Separate Congregationalist from Connecticut, offers an excellent example of one individual in whom the ability to view objectively the conflict between Great Britain and the colonies issued not only in an attack on colonial religious oppression but in a call for spiritual reform as well.

Separate Congregationalists were, like Baptists, products of the Great Awakening. With the Baptists they could not countenance the idea that religious establishments were consistent with the freedom with which Christ made men free. Unlike the Baptists, however, they continued to baptize the infants of professed believers. While their theology followed Edwards' precepts, their positions on the various religious and social controversies of the age mediated between the pro-establishment New Lights and the Baptists. Like both the Baptists and the New Light Congregationalists, Separate Congregationalists like Israel Holly were convinced that the life of the church was to be qualitatively different from the life of the world.

The distinction which Holly saw between church and society came to the fore in his analysis of the Boston Tea Party of December 16, 1773. Eleven days after this affair Holly preached a most unusual sermon on its religious implications for New England. The sermon acknowledged the validity of Whig precepts, but its central theme was divine providence, and its application consisted of a doleful analysis of the colonists' situation, with a stern call for repentance and reform in New England. Throughout the sermon Holly spoke highly of "natural and constitutional liberties," "the natural rights of mankind," and "English liberties" while at the same time denouncing "arbitrary and tyrannical edicts" and "arbitrary power."[9] But the burden of his concern was

---

9. Israel Holly, *God brings about his holy and wise Purpose . . . by using and improving the wicked Dispositions of Mankind in Order thereto . . .* (Hartford: Eben. Watson, 1774), pp. 15, 17, 22, 15, 17.

the divine rather than the human prerogative. His text
(I Kings 12:15) spoke of Rehoboam's loss of the ten tribes
of Israel, a loss which had fulfilled God's plan but which was
also a product of the sinful actions of both Rehoboam and
the ten tribes. Holly felt that it could very well be God's
will that the colonies separate from England in defense of
their just liberties, but that the ruin and destruction inevitably following such a separation should be recognized
as God's punishment for sin in both England and New
England.

The controlling theme of the sermon was not
the Whig view of the justice of the American cause but
the conviction "that God has a wise, holy and righteous
purpose or decree, concerning all events that ever took place."
It was necessary to remember "that in the course of providence God often brings about his purpose or decree concerning particular events, by using and improving the wicked
tempers, and corrupt dispositions of mankind in order thereto."[10] With this perspective, the struggle between England
and the colonies could be viewed impartially and not necessarily in terms of God's side versus the devil's side. The
church, as God's instrument, was not merely to follow the
fashion of the world, but was to judge the world by divine
standards of righteousness.

Holly, at several points in the sermon, stressed
the abstract justice of colonial claims against Great Britain.
He nevertheless argued on religious grounds that colonial
probity in a limited political instance should not blind the
colonists to their susceptibility to God's wrath in other areas:

> If, as we have heard, God brings about his holy and
> wise purpose or decree concerning many particular
> events, by using and improving the wicked dispo-
> sitions of mankind in order thereto, and often im-
> proves the present corruptions of sinners as the means
> to chastise and punish them for former wickedness,
> then we may hence learn what grounds we have to
> fear that God is now about to scourge and chastise,
> in awful severity, our sinful nation and land; and as

10. *Ibid.,* pp. 5, 12.

a just punishment for former sins, to make use of
the present corruptions of men to be the means to
bring about their own misery. How similar the
circumstance of our nation and land now, to that of
Jeroboam and the children of Israel, both with reference to ripeness for judgments by former sins, and
ripeness in present corruptions and wicked dispositions discovered, to be the means to bring mutual ruin
upon our own heads, if heaven prevent not.

On this basis, Holly could make an unusual assessment of
the righteousness of the colonial cause. Although the colonists justly bewailed Great Britain's evil, they had to face
the question: *"Are we better than they?"* To which Holly
confessed: "Must we not with [the apostle] answer, *no in
no wise?"*[11]

If the colonies were due subjects of punishment
because of their sin and in spite of the abstract rectitude
of their contention against Great Britain, then what could
be done? Holly noted that some counseled unity and a con-
certed resistance to the foe, but went on to inquire if such
unity would not be subverted for personal gain by the
grasp of the unscrupulous. No, if the colonies wanted a
way out of their difficulties, they must emulate Nineveh:
*"Break off thy sins by righteousness, and thine eniquities
by shewing mercy to the poor, if it may be a lengthening
of thy tranquility."*[12] New England's sins, though perhaps
not as heinous as England's in an absolute sense, were relatively worse because of God's past favor to that region.

Chief among these sins was the stifling of religious liberty, particularly where fines were imposed and
estates confiscated for exercising the very religious liberty
which "our fore-fathers came into this land, to enjoy." Holly
hoisted the New England establishment with its own Whig
petard:

And yet among other sins, is not New-
England, the government and authority of some of the
colonies in New-England, guilty of exercising the same

11. *Ibid.,* pp. 14, 16.
12. *Ibid.,* p. 20.

> arbitrary power, to abridge many of their natural and constitutional liberties and privileges? . . . But how righteous would it be in God to punish such law-makers, and those who are hardy enough to put the same into execution, by bringing them under arbitrary laws of the same nature?[13]

If New England insisted on addressing Great Britain in the moral tones of absolute right and wrong, New England had best look to itself if it would escape the divine wrath called down upon England for the arbitrary exercise of power, the stifling of religious liberty, and a tyrannous assault on person and goods, for all of these abuses characterized New England's own treatment of religious minorities in its midst.

Holly saw realistically that open conflict with England would bring much sorrow and destruction to the colonies and mother country. He was perhaps overly pessimistic about the prospects for mutual ruin, but his analysis — given the view of providence at the heart of his thought — was a good deal more realistic than much of the heady Patriotism so eager to enlist God for the cause. If God favored the colonies because of the justice of their complaint against Britain, then it must be equally true that God would chastise the colonies if they did not on their part repent of their offenses against God. With this perception, Holly could only advise:

> So now, if we desire the end, viz. the deliverance of this land from the awful judgments with which we are threatened, then let us comply with and be in the use of means requisite, that is, let us repent of sin and turn to God.[14]

Like Isaac Backus, Israel Holly made the distinction between God's righteousness and the righteousness of the American cause. Once having drawn this distinction, Holly, with Backus, was free to call upon Americans to repent of their own evil even while acknowledging the seri-

---

13. *Ibid.,* both quotations from p. 17.
14. *Ibid.,* p. 20.

of the grievances against Great Britain. Holly's re-
d not take the place of his Patriotism, nor did it
distinguishably with that Patriotism. Rather, it transcended the Patriotic impulse in such a way that it participated in Patriotism without being captured by it.

This ability to be at once Patriotic and critical
of American society was not an exclusive property of dissenting bodies such as the Baptists and the Separate Congregationalists. In fact, the clearest illustration of the ability
to maintain the integrity of religious thought in the face of
the Patriotic surge was provided by a pro-establishment New
Light, Samuel Hopkins of Newport, Rhode Island. The intimate connection between religious thinking and socio-
political behavior that characterized the entire period was
a marked feature in the life of this prominent New England
minister who tried to call Revolutionary America to account
for the injustice of slavery.

Hopkins, even more thoroughly than Isaac Backus
and Israel Holly, was a proponent of Jonathan Edwards'
thought. His theological writings stressed the debilitating
nature of human sinfulness and the moral obligation of all
men, even sinners, to love God and honor his law. It was,
however, in the ethical sphere that Hopkins made his most
well known contribution. Taking Edwards' idea that true
virtue consisted in ordering one's action toward any particular object in accordance with that object's true worth,
Hopkins labored to construct an all-encompassing ethical
system. God, because of the infinite goodness of his character, deserved infinite honor. Men, as creatures made in the
image of God, deserved to be treated with the great respect accorded by this high honor. Hopkins' famous ethical
catchword, "disinterested benevolence," was a description
of the way in which individuals should act toward men —
benevolently, because of the high order of divinely created
humanity, and disinterestedly, in consideration of the overarching imperative to honor the other person's inherent
worth. Hopkins' attack on slavery at the time of the Revolu-

tion was deeply rooted in his concept of God and in his belief that human beings, made in God's image, were highly valuable. Like Edwards, Joseph Bellamy, and other New Lights, Hopkins also argued for a sharp distinction between the lost and the saved, for in his view truly benevolent action could issue only from someone who had been renewed by God. Grace was the primary reality; it operated with reliable visibility in the lives of men; the course of ethical decisions in daily life was dependent upon its presence or absence.

Patriotism never became the ultimate moral standard for Hopkins during the Revolutionary era. Rather, Christian benevolence was a higher authority that stood in judgment even over the Whig thought which moved men so mightily in that day. It is not that Hopkins was not himself Patriotic, for as early as the 1750's when he had pastored a church in Great Barrington, Massachusetts, he had argued boldly for colonial rights. But his Patriotic impulse always stood in a relative position on his scale of values. The distinction in his thought between Patriotism and religion was illustrated in a lengthy essay published in 1765 as a response to certain teachings of Jonathan Mayhew. In the preface to this work Hopkins did praise Mayhew for his part in the "controversy with the episcopal party in New England." Hopkins also expressed his belief that Mayhew's work had been very helpful in keeping the colonies out of the clutches of the Church of England. Agreement with Mayhew's political efforts, however, did not stop Hopkins from a thorough dismembering of Mayhew's theology and a forthright counter-presentation of New Light truth.[15] Political kinship could not, in the final analysis, be allowed to hinder the defense of the gospel.

Hopkins' ability to criticize fellow patriots for their neglect of New Light truths, or for their refusal to

15. See Samuel Hopkins, *An Enquiry concerning the Promises of the Gospel . . . Containing, Remarks on two sermons published by Dr. Mayhew . . .* (Boston: W. M'Alpine & J. Fleming, 1765), pp. v-vi for approval of Mayhew's politics, p. 74 for the sharpest disapproval of his theology.

conform to the practices mandated by these truths, was displayed most notably in his ardent attack on the practice of Negro slavery. Proceeding from New Light axioms, he castigated the institution and labored to show how utterly inconsistent it was with the logic of the libertarian ideology justifying separation from Great Britain. His major work on the subject, *A Dialogue, concerning the Slavery of the Africans,* appeared in 1776 and was dedicated to the Continental Congress. The *Dialogue* is a remarkable work, for it indicates that some who did not identify the interests of Christianity and of Patriotism were able, while supporting the colonial cause, to criticize aspects of New England society, based on an overarching Christian conception of social morality.

Hopkins mounted a three-tiered attack on slavery in his *Dialogue*. He first called it to account, in the words of an earlier proposal to finance a Negro mission to Africa, for its "great inhumanity and cruelty."[16] The *Dialogue* itself scored the callous disregard for human life characterizing the slave trade, showed that slaveholding was as morally reprehensible as slave trading, argued that it was hypocrisy to demand return of stolen goods while sanctioning the holding of stolen human beings, and showed how slavery "has a mighty tendency to sink and contract the minds of men, and prevent their making improvements in useful knowledge of any kind."[17] Yet far from dominating his quarrel against slavery, these arguments gave way before a more explicitly Christian assault.

On this second level he called slavery to account as being specifically anti-Christian for its opposition to the external ordinances and exercises of Christianity. The institution, rather than helping to spread the gospel as some claimed, actually hindered its growth; not to cry out against slavery was to run the risk of the judgments pronounced by Jesus on those who did not plead for the oppressed; slave-

16. Samuel Hopkins and Ezra Stiles, "TO THE PUBLIC" [no title given] (n.p.: n.p., n.d. [Newport, 1776]), p. 3.
17. Samuel Hopkins, *A Dialogue concerning the Slavery of the Africans* ... (Norwich: Judah P. Spooner, 1776), pp. 8-11, 15, 37, 44.

holding led to insincere worship of Christ; and Scripture condemned the kind of chattel slavery practiced in the colonies which passed bondage from generation to generation.

On yet a third level, touching the internal substance of the gospel, Hopkins argued that slavery was "very inconsistent . . . with worshipping God thro' Christ." It was a fundamental violation of the principle that all beings created by God were to be accorded treatment as befits their nature. One could not act as a true Christian while treating human beings as beasts. The spirit of the age, Hopkins said, has

> led us to consider [Negroes], not as our brethren, or in any degree on a level with us, but as quite another species of animals, made only to serve us and our children; and as happy in bondage, as in any other state. This has banished all attention to the injustice that is done them, and any proper sense of their misery, or the exercise of benevolence towards them.

In short, if the colonies "had that benevolence, which loves our neighbors as ourselves, and is agreeable to truth and righteousness," they would begin to treat Negroes like fellow human beings and free them from their bonds.[18]

Hopkins' concern for the slaves was not unrelated to his concern for his country. As a New Light he expected to recognize with considerable accuracy the work of God in an individual. With New and Old Lights alike he assumed that the work of God among nations was similarly recognizable. The dedicatory preface of the *Dialogue* praised Congress for its resolution suspending the slave trade in the colonies. As Hopkins read the situation in the second year of the war, God had done "wonderful things" for the colonies "since we have begun to reform the public iniquity [of slave trading]." But it was only to be expected that God's favoring hand would be withdrawn if the colonies did not complete the reformation of this evil by actually freeing the slaves:

---

18. *Ibid.*, first quotation from p. 60; next two from p. 34.

This has been God's usual way of dealing with his professing people; and who can say it is not most reasonable and wise? He then acts the most friendly part to these Colonies and to the masters of slaves, as well as to the slaves themselves, who does his utmost to effect a general emancipation of the *Africans* among us.[19]

Much later, when Hopkins addressed the Providence Society for abolishing the Slave-Trade in 1793, he spoke bitterly of the new United States Constitution which in Art. I, Sec. ii, Par. 3, and Art. I, Sec. ix, Par. 1, had legitimatized not only slaveholding but the blatantly evil slave trade. Considering the favor which God had bestowed upon the United States when it had suspended the slave trade during the war, Hopkins could only foresee a gloomy future as a result of the action of the Constitutional Convention:

When all this is taken into view by the truly pious, who fear God, and believe his word, is it to be wondered at, that their flesh trembleth for fear of the righteous judgment of God? ... Have we not all reason to fear that the vengeance of heaven will fall upon us, as a people in ways perhaps which are not now thought of, unless we repent and reform?[20]

On the basis of his analysis of slavery and the national destiny, Hopkins was able to make much of American reliance on libertarian ideology. Rising above the conventional presentation of the terms of the dispute — in effect, using the Whig world view as a means to accomplish ends determined by a superior system of values — Hopkins reversed the colonial arguments against Great Britain to attack an aspect of colonial society itself. In a series of pointed statements and anguished exclamations, Hopkins articulated some of the sharpest indictments of American moral sense that the eighteenth century would ever hear. Addressing the Congress directly, he points to "the incon-

---

19. *Ibid.*, pp. iv, 54.
20. Samuel Hopkins, *A Discourse upon the Slave-Trade, and the Slavery of the Africans* ... (Providence: J. Carter, 1793), p. 18.

sistence of promoting the slavery of the Africans, at the same time we are asserting our own civil liberty, at the risque of our fortunes and lives." He asks what slaves must think of the rhetorical stance against Great Britain when

> they see the slavery the *Americans* dread as worse than death, is lighter than a feather, compared to their heavy [doom?]; and may be called liberty and happiness, when contrasted with the most abject slavery and unutterable wretchedness to which they are subjected.

His readers are asked to "behold the *sons of liberty,* oppressing and tyrannizing over many thousands of poor blacks, who have as good a claim to liberty as themselves." He shows how all the supposed problems of freeing the slaves would fade like dew in the sun if the "general assemblies, and continental and provincial congresses ... were as much united and engaged in devising ways and means to set at liberty these injured slaves as they are to defend themselves from tyranny." And he calls for God to witness the actions of those who bemoan the British tyranny while continuing to hold slaves:

> Oh, the shocking, the intolerable inconsistence! And this gross, barefaced, practiced inconsistence, is an open, practical condemnation of holding these our brethren in slavery; and in these circumstances the crime of persisting in it becomes unspeakably greater and more provoking in God's sight.[21]

Hopkins concludes the *Dialogue* by inquiring how New Englanders can criticize the Quakers for not coming to the Lord's Supper while they overlook the much more serious offense of treating men made in the image of God like the beasts of the field.

It is important to remember that this fusillade poured forth from engines of war forged in the Great Awakening. Hopkins provides the premier example of the New Light ability to extract itself from the norms of traditional

---

21. Quotations above from *A Dialogue concerning the Slavery of the Africans,* p. iii, p. 30, again p. 30, p. 32, and p. 50.

society with a message at once socially radical and yet grounded in ancient Christian truths. Only someone with an ethical vantage point outside of New England society could call it to account as Hopkins did; only someone who perceived that such distinctions as church and world, regenerate and unregenerate, were of primary reality could have stood in judgment over the norms of his society with standards of a higher authority demanding a more complete obedience.

In a casual remark in the *Dialogue* of 1776, Hopkins said that uniquely national blessings ceased with the passing of the Jewish nation. Virtually isolated from the religiously inclined of his day, Hopkins recognized that "this distinction [of Israel] is now at an end, and all nations are put upon a level; and Christ . . . has taught us to look on all nations as our neighbours and brethren."[22] America was not to be regarded as the New Israel. During the Revolution, the New Light construction of reality which undergirded this recognition was responsible for distinguishing the response of several Edwardseans from that of their ideological and ecclesiastical opponents. A specifically New Light frame of mind also lay behind the ability to distinguish between church and society and to countenance the possibility that colonial traditions and true Christianity might not always have the same ends or be able to employ the same means.

Although Hopkins sounded the clearest call from a religious perspective for reform in Revolutionary America, he was not alone. Levi Hart of Preston, Connecticut, spoke out with Hopkins against slavery in a tract published in 1775, *Liberty Described and Recommended*. Like Hopkins, Hart thought it odd for colonists to protest British "tyranny" so vociferously while winking at chattel slavery in the colonies. Hart was the son-in-law of Joseph Bellamy, the leader with Hopkins of the Edwardsean New Divinity in New England. Hart was also a Patriot. For him as for Hopkins, however, that Patriotism was not to be confused with the need to evaluate

---

22. *Ibid.,* p. 21.

and critique the colonists themselves during the struggle against Great Britain.

An even more striking application of religious principles in the Revolutionary situation was provided by a Presbyterian from New Jersey, Jacob Green. Green is particularly important in showing that religiously derived criticism of the colonies was not restricted to New England Congregationalism. He is also important in that he participated more directly in Patriotic activities than Backus, Holly, Hopkins, or Hart.

Green, as was mentioned in Chapter Three, rendered stalwart service to the Patriot cause: his zealous defense of colonial rights led to his selection as a delegate to the first Provincial Congress in New Jersey; he opened his home as winter headquarters for officers from Washington's army and as a hospital for released prisoners of war; and he labored to convince colonial public opinion of the justice of Patriotism and the propriety of independence. In 1776 he published a well-reasoned plea against efforts to reconcile Great Britain and the colonies, and in the difficult days of the war he took to the public press to encourage those grown weary in the fight. He treated the religious dimension of the American struggle at greater length in a fast-day sermon of April, 1778.

Green's conception of the conflict was made up of the standard Whig elements. His newspaper articles, for example, rang with the praise of "the glorious cause of *Liberty* [and] . . . the natural rights of mankind," they defied the British design to reduce the colonies "to a state of mean and abject slavery," and they proclaimed that "Liberty is given us by God."[23] Green accepted wholeheartedly the Whig world view with its picture of British corruption, its exaltation of God-given liberty and natural rights, its fear of governmental conspiracies leading to tyrannical slavery, and its conjunction of civil and religious liberties.

23. Jacob Green, *Documents Relating to the Revolutionary History of the State of New Jersey,* ed. William Nelson, Vol. IV (Trenton: State Gazette Publishing Co., 1914), 344.

Green's religious analysis of the crisis operated, however, more often on its own terms than as support for Real Whiggery. His fast-day sermon illustrates the connection he saw between religious and political aspects of the situation:

> While I am obliged to point out many crying sins among us, I cannot help animating you from the consideration that we are engaged in a glorious cause. In this cause I would have you encouraged and emboldened, though I must lead your thoughts to some disagreeable subjects. There are sins among us. God is angry and contending with us.[24]

While no doubt existed in Green's mind concerning the justice of the American cause, he could indict the colonists themselves for contradicting the Whig standards by which the British were measured and, more importantly, for violating the revealed will of God.

Both Green's religious commitments and his willingness to let the Whig sword cut against Britons *and* colonials came to his assistance when he called colonial society to repentance and reformation. Like Holly, Green urged an end to ecclesiastical establishments in America because of their incompatibility with civil liberty and with the freedom which a true response to the gospel required. He also used the Revolutionary crisis as a means to call for a revival of true religion. The fact that "not merely the sabbath, but religious people and religious exercises are treated with contempt" proved to Green that the colonists were not repenting in the face of evidences of God's displeasure revealed through the hardships of the war.[25]

The focus of Green's denunciation of colonial society was the practice of Negro slavery. Slavery, a "most cruel, inhuman, unnatural sin," was indicted on at least four counts that intermingled Whig and Christian moral standards: (1) slavery violated God's commandment to love one's neigh-

---

24. Jacob Green, *A Sermon . . . of public Fasting and Prayer . . .* (Chatham, N.J.: Shepard Kollock, 1779), p. 5.
25. *Ibid.,* p. 9.

bor as one's self; (2) it unjustly placed in bondage people who had never forfeited their right to freedom; (3) it interdicted the natural and unalienable right to freedom; and (4) it was condemned by the apostle Paul who ranked man-stealing with murder.[26] Slavery thus violated the best standards of human and divine morality.

Like Hopkins, Green saw tremendous irony in the combination of protests against Britain's enslavement of the colonies and the toleration of chattel servitude: "What a dreadful absurdity! What a shocking consideration, that people who are so strenuously contending for liberty, should at the same time encourage and promote slavery!"[27] Furthermore:

> What foreign nation can believe that we who so loudly complain of Britain's attempts to oppress and enslave us, are, at the same time, voluntarily holding multitudes of fellow creatures in abject slavery; and that while we are abundantly declaring that we esteem liberty the greatest of all earthly blessings.[28]

Perhaps because of his more active participation in colonial politics, Green was somewhat more optimistic than Hopkins about the future of the Americans. He thought that the colonies would probably succeed in gaining independence from Britain, for even the evil of slavery could not hide the vile conduct of Great Britain toward its American possessions. Green also thought that the colonies might prosper in a material way after the war because of their great resources. Nevertheless, the stain of slavery would be a blot and a mark of shame upon the new nation:

> However we may be free from British oppression, I venture to say, we shall have inward convulsions, contentions, oppressions, and various calamities, so that our liberty will be uncomfortable, till we wash our hands from the guilt of negro slavery.[29]

26. *Ibid.*, p. 14.
27. Jacob Green, *Observations: On the Reconciliation of Great-Britain; and the Colonies* . . . (Philadelphia: Robert Bell, 1776), p. 29n.
28. *Sermon of public Fasting*, p. 12.
29. *Ibid.*, p. 16.

Like Backus, Holly, Hopkins, and Hart, Jacob Green adhered to the basic Puritan theology as it had been refurbished by Jonathan Edwards. This small group of Edwardseans was not unique in preserving the integrity of religious convictions during the Revolution, for Christians from other traditions also called for an end to slavery or demanded an end to the legal establishment of religion in the colonies. These Edwardseans, however, did constitute a most unusual class among those who self-consciously honored the Puritan forefathers and who professed to represent the Reformed faith in America. Where other Calvinistic ministers felt no qualms about intermingling the verities of political liberty and the truths of Christian freedom, these individuals preserved a distinction between the two. All of them proved in the end to be faithful, in one degree or another, to the cause of colonial Patriotism. None of them, however, allowed that loyalty to displace a more intense loyalty to the Christian faith as they understood it. Nor did it push aside their deeply felt obligation to speak specifically Christian truth into Revolutionary society.

V   *The Loyalist Response*

The study of colonial Americans who remained loyal to Great Britain during the Revolution has only recently received serious attention. For a very long time, those writing on American history perceived the Revolution in much the same terms as the original Patriots. So long as the virtue of the Patriot cause and the magnitude of British evil were accepted without question, the historian could only look upon colonial Tories as the sadly deluded, stubbornly obnoxious, and crassly self-serving lackeys of the British tyrants. From a religious perspective likewise, belief in the manifest Christian righteousness of the Patriot effort prevented later Americans from being able to understand how a colonist could be both a genuine believer and a Tory. Although a definitive treatment of Christian Loyalists in the American Revolution must await the results of wide-ranging and comprehensive studies yet to be published, enough evidence exists to sketch an intriguing picture of many Americans who, for implicit or explicit Christian reasons, resisted Patriotism and maintained allegiance to Great Britain.

The motives which led colonial Americans to remain loyal to Britain were as many and varied as those prompting advocacy of independence. In all, one-fifth to one-third of the colonists are thought to have harbored Tory leanings or to have actively supported the British ministry. The positions of some, particularly crown officials and Anglican ministers, predisposed them to Loyalism. Some were tied

to England by commercial, family, or traditional ties. Some
were convinced through reading the volumes of political
writings of the day that the argument for Loyalism was
intrinsically better than the case for rebellion. And many
were simply indisposed by their own constitutions to the
distress, social upheaval, and radical changes entailed by
the Revolution. From a religious point of view, Christian
Loyalists divide naturally between members of the Church
of England and the other religious bodies in the colonies.

Anglicans, like most colonial groups, differed
among themselves in approaching the struggle for independence. Although many Anglicans in the middle and southern
colonies supported the Patriot cause — George Washington
and Patrick Henry, for example, belonged to the Church of
England — the most vocal Anglican commentators on the
the war were Loyalists from New York and New England.
Anglican dissenters from Patriotism were by their position
as members of *the* Church of England conspicuous in their
Loyalism, and they have left a fuller record of their thinking
on the subject than Loyalists from other communions.

Many examples could be cited to show the sincere Christian convictions displayed by members of the
Church of England who resisted the drive for independence.
Among these Loyalists were such laymen as Cadwallader
Colden, Jr., of New York, son of that colony's former lieutenant governor. Colden wrote in August, 1777, that he was
unable to take the oath of allegiance to the newly independent state of New York. He admits that it was a great
temptation to swear allegiance to the new provincial government and consequently to live out the war unmolested
on his country estate and at peace with his Whig neighbors.
Nevertheless, he refused to subscribe and prayed daily not
to be "Led into [the] Temptation" of violating his conscience on this matter. In Colden's eyes, his situation could
be reduced to this choice: "Shall I now to Avoid a Little
temperary Uneasyness and Inconveniency, Give the Lye to
all my former Conduct and even appeal to the Majesty of

Heaven to Confirm this Lye?" His answer was to the point: "God forbid!"[1]

Earlier, in 1776, the Rev. John Beach of Newton, Connecticut, had refused the order of local Whigs to stop saying the prayers for George III included in the Anglican liturgy. When Beach's refusal became public knowledge, angry Patriots forcibly dragged him from his church and threatened to cut out his tongue. In this hour of trial Beach spoke these words in what he thought would be his last audible prayer: "O Lord and Father of mercies, look upon these mine enemies and forgive them. They know not what they do, they are blindly misled. O God, in mercy open their eyes."[2] Unexpectedly, this show of piety softened the Patriot hearts and Beach was released. Other Anglicans did not get off so lightly.

Among those who paid a sterner penalty was Moses Dunbar, whose last days on the earth constituted one of the most notable examples of Christian fortitude witnessed on either side during the Revolutionary period. Dunbar, a layman from Waterbury, Connecticut, had been converted from Congregationalism to Anglicanism before 1776, and at the start of the war he had offered his services to the British. In January, 1777, during a visit to his home in Connecticut, he was captured by Patriot forces with a captain's commission from a British regiment in his pocket. A Hartford jury sentenced him to death by hanging. On the day before his execution Dunbar wrote this simple letter to his children:

> My Children: Remember your creator in the days of your youth. Learn your Creed, the Lord's Prayer, and the Ten Commandments and catechism, and go to church as often as you can, and prepare yourselves as soon as you are of a proper age to worthily partake of the Lord's Supper. I charge you all, never leave the church. Read the Bible. Love the Saviour wherever you may be.

---

1. In *The Price of Loyalty: Tory Writings from the Revolutionary Era,* ed. Catherine S. Crary (New York: McGraw-Hill, 1973), pp. 205-206.
2. *Ibid.,* p. 107.

On that same day Dunbar also wrote a longer personal statement under the title "Last Speech and Dying Words." This document spoke briefly of his early life, mentioned the family estrangement caused by his conversion to the Church of England, related his inability to "reconcile my Opinion to the necessity or Lawfulness of taking up Arms against Great Britain," gave the details of his arrest and trial, and then took up spiritual matters:

> I shall soon be delivered from all the Pains & Troubles of this Mortal State, I shall be Answerable to None but the allseeing God, who is infinitely Just & who knoweth all things. As I am fully persuaded that I depart in a State of peace with God & my own Conscience, I can have but little doubt of my future Happiness thro' the Mercy of God & Merits of Jesus Christ. I have sincerely repented of my sins, Examined my Heart, prayed Earnestly to God for Mercy for the Gracious pardon of my Manifold & heinous Sins, & now resign myself wholly to the disposal of my heavenly Father, submitting my will to his.
>
> From the very Bottom of my heart I forgive all my Enemies, and Earnestly pray to God to forgive them all. . . .
>
> I die in the Possession and Communion of the Church of England. . . .
>
> My last advice to you is that you, above all other Concerns, prepare yourselves (with God's Assistance) for yr future, Eternal State. You will all shortly be as near Eternity as I *now* am & will then view both worldly and Spiritual things in the same Light in which I do *now* view them. You will then see all worldly Things to be but Shadows, but Vapours, but Vanity of Vanities; and the Things of the Spiritual World to be of importance beyond all Discription. You will then be sensible that the Pleasures of a Good Conscience & the Happiness of a near Prospect of Heaven infinitely outway all the Riches, Pleasures & Honor of this Mean, sinfull World.
>
> God the Father, God the Son, God the Holy Ghost, have mercy upon me & receive my Spirit. Amen! Amen![3]

---

3. *Ibid.,* pp. 231, 232, 233-234.

By no means were all Anglicans required to face the hangman for their loyalty to Great Britain. Dunbar's testimony, however, does suggest that profound Christian convictions were not restricted to the Patriotic side.

Anglicans did not suffer in silence as the war approached and the first skirmishing took place. A large-scale attack against the Patriotic arguments had proceeded on many fronts long before the outbreak of hostilities. While most of the argumentation produced by churchmen remained in the strictly political sphere, much was also imbued with explicitly Christian content. Anglicans countered the Patriotic arguments with four general theses: (1) that the English monarchical system was a distinctly better form of government than the democratic republicanism proposed by the Patriots; (2) that individuals had a moral, indeed a Christian, obligation to submit to their lawful rulers and to obey their laws; (3) that inviolable oaths sworn by Anglican clergymen prevented any tampering with the church's liturgy in order to appease Patriotic scruples; and (4) that the Bible explicitly condemned the kind of actions taken by the Patriots.

The Loyalists, some of whom did share general Whig conceptions about the nature of governmental power, simply were unable to believe that the threat of "slavery" from Parliament or the established Episcopal Church could at all be compared to the dangers from a popular mob run amok into unregulated anarchy. The Rev. Henry Caner of King's Chapel in Boston observed the agitation and unrest being stirred up over the tea tax of 1773 and wrote to the Royal Governor of New Hampshire: "Such are the Effects of popular Gov^{rmt}, Sedition, Anarchy, & Violence, & all this flame kindled & kept alive by about 1/2 doz. men of bad principles & morals."[4] After actual fighting had broken out, Miles Cooper, the second president of King's College (later Columbia University) wrote less passionately:

> When once they ["the People"] conceive the governed to be superior to the Governors and that

---

4. *Ibid.,* p. 19.

they may set up their pretended Natural Rights in Opposition to the positive law of the state, they will naturally proceed to despise dominion and speak evil of dignities and to open a door for Anarchy, confusion, and every evil work to enter.[5]

Samuel Seabury, who cared for an upstate New York parish during the war and who afterwards became the first bishop of the Protestant Episcopal Church in America, issued a series of reasoned tracts which sought to expose the intrinsic weakness of colonial political aspirations and to remind the colonies of the inherent strengths of the British system which the Patriots were rushing to throw over. His tract, *Free Thoughts on the Proceedings of the Continental Congress,* dealt with basic political issues but also suggested that Christian belief itself could very well become a casualty of the spirit of independence sweeping the land.

In its most extreme form, this line of argument held that the Presbyterians and Congregationalists only wanted to throw off the rightful sovereignty of the king in order to foment open rebellion and despotism. More typically Anglican, however, were the arguments of Charles Inglis, rector of Trinity Church in New York City, who took up his pen against Thomas Paine's *Common Sense* in order to argue that monarchy was the simplest and most stable form of government and that democracy was an untried system subject to unknown disorders.

In his tract directed against Paine, *The True Interest of America Stated,* Inglis also intimated the positive ideal which Anglicans advanced as a counter to the Patriotic vision. More of the specifically Christian content of Anglican social theory emerged in this emphasis than in the strictly political debate. A recent historian of the Loyalists, William A. Nelson, has described this Anglican social ideal as "the lost catholic world of Hooker." That is, Anglicans such as Inglis or Jonathan Boucher of Maryland looked back to the world envisioned in Richard Hooker's *Laws of Ecclesiastical*

---

5. In Raymond W. Albright, *A History of the Protestant Episcopal Church* (New York: Macmillan, 1964), p. 116.

Polity, the great apologetic work for the regularization of religion in the sixteenth century under Elizabeth. From this perspective, life in *society* was to reflect divinely constituted order as much as life for *individuals.* The orders of society, the traditional patterns of authority, the very inequalities of place and station, did not exist to satisfy base human lusts but to reflect God's plan and purpose for Christian life in society. Nelson summarizes well the contrast of the Anglican and the Patriot world views: Boucher, Inglis, and others like them had

> seen a vision of a world where society was blessed, and man could be saved, not by seeking his own fulfill-ment only, but by living in grace with his fellows. The revolutionists, on the other hand, . . . had little interest in society as such. It was the life of the individual that was sacred to them and their theories about society were usually mere projections of their concern for the individual. Conceiving of society almost as a machine, they were eager to learn its secrets, to dismantle it if necessary and rebuild it on rational principles.[6]

All the talk of natural rights, British tyranny, and a grasping Church of England appeared to these Anglicans as transparent excuses to throw over the traces of civilization and to embark on a social bacchanal that could only end in destruction, confusion, and the death of Christian culture. From this point of view, the Christian rationale for Patri-otism seemed very shaky indeed. The Rev. Simon Baxter's notorious sermon "Tyrannicide Proved Lawful," in which the assassination of George Washington and other Patriot leaders was deemed honorable, also contained a sharp criti-cism of the supposed Christian integrity of the Patriots. In this sermon, preached late in the war after the Continental Congress had sealed the alliance with France, Baxter reflected on the irony that colonial protesters against the Quebec Act were now welcoming French aid as a means to defeat Protestant England:

---

6. William H. Nelson, *The American Tory* (Oxford: Oxford University Press, 1961), pp. 186, 187.

> You began rebellion, because your King
> would not persecute, but tolerate his faithful Catholic
> subjects in Canada, and, to support your rebellion, you
> have since joined yourselves unto idols, and made al-
> legiance with the Papists of France, to root up the
> protestant religion, for which our fathers bled and died.[7]

To more moderate Anglican Loyalists, no less than to ardent
Tories like Baxter, it was inexplicable how colonists could
in good conscience toss over the stable and tested traditions
of the English system for the flux and instability of an
untried democratic republicanism. It was even more astound-
ing that this outrage could be defended in Christian terms.

Beyond their inability to grasp the logic of the
Patriot cause, members of the Church of England also
thought that all men, and Christians in particular, had a
moral obligation to submit to the rulers which God had
provided for them. Writing before the war itself in 1774,
Thomas Bradbury Chandler of Elizabethtown, New Jersey,
the most articulate colonial proponent for the establishment
of an American bishop, expressed his conviction that the allegiance of a subject to a properly constituted government
was not an optional matter:

> The principles of submission and all lawful
> authority are as inseparable from a sound, genuine
> member of the Church of England, as any religious
> principle whatever. The Church has always been famed
> and respected for its *loyalty*, and its regard to order
> and government.[8]

After the actual outbreak of fighting, many Anglicans fled
the country rather than submit to what they considered an
illegally constituted government. One of those who left was
Isaac Wilkins, an influential member of the New York colonial legislature. Wilkins was a faithful lay member of the
Church of England who became a minister in the American

---

7. In *The Price of Loyalty*, p. 222.
8. Thomas Bradbury Chandler, *A Friendly Address to All Reasonable
Americans, on the Subject of our Political Confusions* ... (New York:
James Rivington, 1774), p. 51.

Protestant Episcopal Church long after the war's end. His religious sentiments were clearly expressed, however, at a much earlier date as in these words written in 1775 upon his departure from the country:

> It has been my constant maxim through life to do my duty conscientiously and to trust the issue of my actions to the Almighty. . . . I leave America and every endearing connection because I will not raise my hand against my Sovereign, nor will I draw my sword against my Country.[9]

For many Anglicans in the colonies, Loyalism was more than a mere convenience. It was rather an outgrowth of the conviction that Christianity demanded allegiance to one's ruler and obedience to his laws.

A third motivation inspiring Loyalism pertained more directly to Anglican clergymen serving in the colonies. In assuming their clerical offices, ministers of the Church of England swore not to countenance any effort to depose or harm the English sovereign. In addition, the stated services of the Anglican liturgy contained specific prayers for the king and his family which the priest was sworn to include in the regular services of the church. The dilemma faced by Anglican curates, particularly in New England where the "missionaries" of the Society for the Propagation of the Gospel were often engaged in long-term struggles with the local religious establishments, was summarized with particular clarity by E. Edwards Beardsley, the author of a nineteenth-century history of the Episcopal Church in Connecticut:

> As faithful Missionaries of the Venerable Society [the SPG], from which came their chief support, they honestly believed themselves bound by their oaths of allegiance, taken at the time of their ordination, to pray for the Sovereign whose dominion the colonies had thrown off; and guided by the forms of the Liturgy, they could omit no part in conducting

---

9. In *The Price of Loyalty*, p. 35.

public worship without doing violence to their own consciences.[10]

Demands by the Patriots to repudiate these vows drove many curates, who may have had some sympathy for the Revolution, into an unreserved defense of Loyalism.

A convention of Connecticut Anglicans meeting in late July, 1776 decided that since they were bound by oath to the Book of Common Prayer and its prayers for the king, since they could amend the church's forms of worship only by an act of sacrilege, and since they would bring "Suspension, Excommunication, and Deposition" down upon their heads by altering the church's liturgy, they would abstain from reading Communion and the other services contained in the Book of Common Prayer. In their churches they would merely read the Bible, homilies, and pious tracts without holding official services. In New Brunswick, New Jersey, Abraham Beach closed his church completely rather than alter the forms of the liturgy referring to the king.

The clearest expression of the moral obligation felt by many Anglican ministers to uphold their vows was made by William Clark of Dedham, Massachusetts, on Easter Sunday, 1777. The Massachusetts assembly had legislated a fifty pound fine for praying for King George or advocating allegiance to him. Clark announced his intention to cease holding services in the church until changes could be made in the liturgy or until the laws of the new state of Massachusetts could be modified. He then elaborated upon the reasons which led him to this step:

> By vows, oaths, and subscriptions which have been made on Earth and recorded in heaven I am obliged to act as a dutiful subject of His most Gracious Majesty, King George the Third, and to the constant use of the Liturgy of that Church of which under God he is the head.... There are various expressions in this liturgy which plainly discountenance all kinds of rebellion and opposition to his Kingly Government, and the very naming of him as our most gra-

10. E. Edwards Beardsley, *The History of the Episcopal Church in Connecticut,* 4th ed. (Boston: Houghton Mifflin, 1883), Vol. I, 315.

cious Sovereign, is I suppose sufficient to break the law [of Massachusetts]. To give up these petitions or prayers while I use the other prayers is against the present light of my conscience. Both my oath of allegiance (which neither the Congress, however respectable in their personal characters, nor the Pope himself can absolve me from ...) and my solemnly subscribing to use the Liturgy strongly unite to oblige me to pray for the King's majesty till such time as he shall be pleased to relinquish his right of Government or jurisdiction over these Colonies. Then and not till then I shall think myself lawfully and properly absolved from my oath of allegiance, and all obligations arising from my subscription will fall of course.[11]

The religious obligation to fulfill solemn oaths left many Anglican ministers with no choice but Loyalism when local or state regulations mandated a change in the order of the Anglican service.

Direct arguments from Scripture were not as frequent from Loyalist ministers as from preachers who backed the Patriotic effort, but the Bible did play a significant role in Anglican Loyalism. In 1774 Thomas Bradbury Chandler argued on the basis of Romans 13 that the Apostle Paul had demanded submission even to the worst of tyrants, Nero. Paul knew what he was talking about, Chandler felt, for "the bands of society would be dissolved, the harmony of the world confounded, and the order of nature subverted, if reverence, respect, and obedience might be refused to those whom the constitution has vested with the highest authority."[12]

Jonathan Boucher of Maryland was another Anglican who discovered a foundation for Loyalism in the Bible. In a sermon "On Civil Liberty, Passive Obedience, and Nonresistance" preached in 1775, Boucher argued that the "liberty" of Galatians 5:1 did not signify political self-determination, as Patriotic preachers blithely assumed, but rather, release from the dominion of sin. The New Testament did, however, speak clearly of political obligations in

11. In Walter Herbert Stowe, "A Study in Conscience: Some Aspects of the Relations of the Clergy to the State," *Historical Magazine of the Protestant Episcopal Church,* XIX (December, 1950), 309.
12. *A Friendly Address,* p. 5.

demanding "obedience to the laws of every country, in every kind or form of government." "Obedience to Government is every man's duty," Boucher went on, "because it is every man's interest; but it is particularly incumbent on Christians, because . . . it is enjoined by the positive commands of God." He argued specifically that true freedom involved mainly the liberty to obey laws proposed by one's properly constituted authorities. To support his contention Boucher cited specific biblical injunctions to submit to the state. He adduced Titus 3:1 ("Put them in mind to be subject to principalities and powers, to obey magistrates, to be ready to every good work") as merely one of the many texts which indicated the importance which submission to lawful authorities held for the apostle Paul. After an examination of the New Testament evidence, Boucher concluded that "the duty of submission and obedience to Government was enjoined on the converts to Christianity with new and stronger sanctions."[13]

Anglican Loyalism was the most consistent phenomenon joining Christian convictions and anti-Patriotism during the Revolutionary period. Members of the Church of England who maintained allegiance to Great Britain did so for many different reasons, but Christian convictions were as important in their Loyalism as they were in the Christian republicanism proclaimed by many Patriots. The desire to live both as good citizens and as true Christians was one very important motive undergirding the defense of monarchy, submissiveness to the English government, fidelity to oaths, and the use of Scripture in the service of Loyalism.

Members of the Church of England were by no means the only American Christians to remain loyal to Great Britain during the Revolutionary period. Although no other denomination manifested a Loyalist perspective as consistently as the Church of England, other Christian groups also harbored significant Loyalist sentiment. Unlike the record

---

13. Jonathan Boucher, *A View of the Causes and Consequences of the American Revolution; in Thirteen Discourses, Preached in North America between the years 1763 and 1775* . . . (London: G. G. and J. Robinson, 1797), pp. 503-506.

of Anglican Loyalism, however, the activities of Tories in other denominations have not received extensive documentation. The pioneering student of American Loyalism in the nineteenth century, Lorenzo Sabine, offered this account for the failure of Loyalists in general to leave behind a significant body of records:

> Men who, like the Loyalists, separate themselves from their friends and kindred, who are driven from their homes, who surrender the hopes and expectations of life, and who become outlaws, wanderers, and exiles — such men leave few memorials behind them. Their records are scattered and lost, and their very names pass from human recollection.[14]

In spite of the difficulties that have attended the retention and use of primary historical data concerning the Loyalists, sufficient evidence exists to show that many Christians outside of the Church of England shared the Loyalist perspective.

It is not surprising that significant Loyalist sentiment existed among Methodists, who at the time of the Revolution were still a fledgling body in America. From England American Methodists received word of Charles Wesley's openly stated belief in the doctrines of divine right and passive obedience. John Wesley, for his part, expressed public sympathy for the inequities inflicted upon the colonies; but he also criticized American Whigs for their highly inflated prattle about the "slavery" resulting from British policies and for their disobedience of the clear scriptural injunction to be subject for the sake of conscience to the powers that be. In seeking to put British wrongs against Americans in their proper light, Wesley reminded his American friends that the true slaves in the colonies were the Negroes in chattel bondage. He also cited himself as an example of an Englishman who, because he lacked the requisite property qualification, was not able to vote in Parliamentary elections and who, therefore, paid taxes without representation.

---

14. Lorenzo Sabine, *Biographical Sketches of Loyalists of the American Revolution, with An Historical Essay* (Boston: Little, Brown, 1864), Vol. I, iii.

Because of the wide publicity given to the Wesleys' opinions on the conflict, Methodists in America were suspected of Toryism. Indeed, many of the Methodist missionaries in America probably shared their leaders' political sentiments. Whether they agreed or not, all of the English missionaries except Francis Asbury returned to the mother country during the war. Asbury, who shared a Patriotic sense of outrage at British imperial policies, did not hide his displeasure over Wesley's comments on the political crisis. Due at least in part to Asbury's rejection of Wesley's Toryism, Methodists were able to resume their rapid advances in America after the war while other Loyalist bodies, particularly the Anglicans, suffered long under the stigma of Toryism. The less well known Methodists in Revolutionary America who harkened to the logic of Wesley's political views and who left America during the conflict included both Englishmen such as George Shadford, who served as a missionary in America from 1773 to 1777, and native Americans such as Benjamin Abbott, who was born on Long Island and who pastored Methodist groups in New York and New Jersey from 1773 until the war.

The Methodists were still a very small body at the time of the Revolution. Such Loyalism as was found in their ranks owed much to their strong ties with England and their deference to the opinions of the Wesleys. Methodist Loyalism is of particular significance insofar as it was grounded in the specifically biblical approach to the conflict taken by John Wesley, for, as we have noted, it was far more common in colonial America for biblical arguments to fall in behind Whig Patriotism than behind British Loyalism.

Other small denominations also harbored significant amounts of Loyalism. The Roman Catholic Church, a relatively insignificant religious force in the colonial era whose period of great growth still lay some forty to fifty years in the future, contributed some sympathizers to the British side. Colonial Catholics had several reasons for becoming Loyalists: the Quebec Act seemed to indicate a greater willingness on the part of Great Britain to tolerate Roman

Catholics; the hostility of American Protestants to the Catholics seemed as bad as, or even worse than, that of the English; and the structure and practice of Roman Catholicism in the eighteenth century still fostered a deference to officially established authority, whether in church or state.

Another group that maintained its loyalty to Great Britain was the Sandemanians, or Glasites, of New England. This small sect had arisen in England early in the eighteenth century under a former Presbyterian minister, John Glas. A number of adherents had been won to this group in New England by Glas's son-in-law, Robert Sandeman. Glas and Sandeman taught a strictly literal application of the Bible and an almost exclusive focus on faith in religious matters. For his extreme stand, Sandeman was criticized as an Antinomian by both New and Old Lights in New England. The group's strict adherence to a literalistic interpretation of the Bible predisposed it against Patriotism, because the Patriots resisted the powers ordained by God. In addition, the harshness with which Sandemanians had been treated in New England by both civil and religious authorities left no doubt in their minds that the tyranny of Parliament was less odious than the burdens imposed by the New England establishment. The Sandemanians, unlike the Methodists and Roman Catholics, never became a significant religious force in America. Their Loyalism nevertheless provides an interesting sidelight in the study of Christianity during the Revolutionary period.

Among the "Patriotic denominations" — Congregationalists, Presbyterians, and, to a lesser extent, Baptists — the advocates of an independent United States, of a Christian republic, were so numerous and so vocal that it is easy to receive the false impression that none of the members of these denominations were Loyalists. There was, however, significant Loyalist sentiment in each of these denominations.

Some Baptists, whose doubts concerning the initial break with Great Britain were examined in Chapter Four, also doubted the rectitude of the American cause after the outbreak of hostilities. It is difficult to reconstruct the exact reasons for Baptist Loyalism since records are spotty and since the Baptist Loyalists were often laymen who did not leave written accounts of their decisions. In New England, a few Baptists joined the British forces under Burgoyne at the battle of Bennington in April, 1777. The sons of Baptist elder Clark Rogers of Hancock, Massachusetts, sided with the Tories, and two Baptist elders in Newport, Rhode Island, refused to sign a loyalty oath to the independent colony in July, 1776. Whether Baptist Loyalism in New England arose out of reaction to Congregationalist strictures upon Baptist life or from specifically scriptural insights into the nature of civil strife is not clear. Similarly, the nature of the Loyalism of the Philadelphia Baptist, Morgan Edwards, is also unclear. Edwards was a leading Baptist missionary, preacher, and organizer in eastern Pennsylvania during the Revolutionary period. When the days arrived which, in Tom Paine's words, tried the souls of men, Edwards opted for loyalty to Great Britain. He may have been led to this step through his contacts with Philadelphia's Quakers or he may have taken it for other political or religious reasons. Whatever the case, Edwards was probably the most well known of the small, but not insignificant, number of Baptists in America who cast their lot with the mother country.

The sources of Loyalism within the Presbyterian and Congregational denominations are somewhat clearer; but here again, Loyalists have not received the intensive scholarship that has made possible a fuller understanding of the nature of Christian Patriotism. Several of the very motives which turned Anglicans from Patriotism also influenced ministers and laymen within the more Patriotic groups. Among the Presbyterians, who were perhaps the most thoroughly Patriotic of American denominations, Loyalism arose from an unwillingness to break oaths sworn to the British monarch, from an uneasiness concerning the legality of the Patriot revolt, and from an unwillingness to throw over the Christian obligation to submit to proper rulers.

In the first instance, Scottish settlers in North Carolina resisted the logic of Patriotism because of oaths sworn to the English king. These Scottish settlers, among whom were at least some Presbyterians, had sworn fidelity to George II after the Battle of Culloden in 1745. Their immigration to the new world did not lessen the obligation these Scots felt to their oaths. As in virtually all decisions in the colonies affecting the disposition to loyalty, other factors also influenced these Scottish settlers. Before the Revolutionary War, they had constituted a segment of the Regulators, the group of frontiersmen who organized resistance to the colonial aristocracy on North Carolina's eastern shore. When that aristocracy opted for the colonial cause during the Revolution, the Regulators, including the Scottish Presbyterians among them, retained their allegiance to Great Britain.

The most prominent Presbyterian Loyalist in the colonies had other reasons for resisting the Patriotic surge. John Joachim Zubly, a native Swiss, had been the first minister of the Independent Presbyterian Church of Savannah, Georgia. Zubly, unlike many Loyalists, shared Whig principles in abstract political matters. He denounced taxation without representation during the Stamp Act controversy and argued for significant checks and balances on the exercise of royal and Parliamentary power. He did not, however, see the republican alternative to the English system in as favorable terms as the colonial Patriots did. With a deep commitment to the necessity of legal sanctions in political affairs and a firm belief in the folly of rapid, unthinking change in government, Zubly was unwilling to endorse colonial independence even as he argued for the redress of colonial grievances. Because of the Whig sentiments expressed in such works as his *Law of Liberty,* a sermon preached in 1775 at the opening of the Georgia Provincial Congress, Zubly was named as a member of the Georgia delegation to the Continental Congress. He participated in this body until he sensed that Congress favored independence over the correction of problems within the British system. For this reason he left the Congress early in 1776 and returned to Georgia. The Georgia Provincial Legislature banished him in 1777 and confiscated half of his goods. Until his death in July, 1781, Zubly engaged in a haphazard ministry among the slaves and wherever his Loyalism did not deprive him of a pulpit. For his rejection of the idea of independence and his adherence to a value system which was unable to violate standards of British legality, this noted Presbyterian minister received in return only hardship, disdain, and discomfort.

Among Presbyterians of the middle colonies, the Christian Patriotism of President John Witherspoon was much more influential than the Loyalism of Zubly. Yet even here a few Presbyterians refused to follow the Patriotic majority and remained loyal to Britain. When William Smith, a Presbyterian layman from New York, was called before the Council of Safety, his reasons for remaining loyal to the king included some of the points which other Christians had also raised in objection to independence:

> I said that I considered myself as a Subject of King Geo: III of Great Britain and a Member of the old or British Government. That I never thought the Seperation justifiable — That Resistance to Governmt. could never be innocent unless there was great Oppression & Revolution practicable and the Remedy sure — That the Evils brought on by Opposition being great there ought to be a Moral Certainty of [their] being less than those which were induced.[15]

Sources of Congregationalist Loyalism also tended to be more political and constitutional than explicitly biblical. The prominence given to such Patriotic Congregational ministers as Jonathan Mayhew, Charles Chauncy, and Ezra Stiles obscures the fact that many other Congregational ministers remained faithful to king and Parliament. Even in Connecticut, where Congregational support for the Patriot cause was almost unanimous, an occasional voice opposed the Whig tide. John Smalley, minister of New Britain's First Church, for example, thought at the outbreak of hostilities that the people of Massachusetts were "guilty of downright rebellion against Majesty itself." As Connecticut armed to go to the aid of Boston, Smalley could only expostulate in wonder: "What! Will you fight against your King?"[16]

---

15. In "Presbyterians and the American Revolution: A Documentary Account," *Journal of Presbyterian History,* LII (Winter, 1974), 430.
16. In Epaphroditus Peck, *The Loyalists of Connecticut* (New Haven: Yale University Press, 1934), p. 3.

Loyalist sentiment among Congregationalists north of Connecticut was even more widespread. Some degree of Loyalist commitment could be found from Boston in the east (the Revs. Mather Byles and Ebenezer Pemberton) to Pittsfield in the west (the lawyer Woodbridge Little); from Deerfield in the south (the Rev. Jonathan Ashley) to Kittery, Maine, in the north (the Rev. Benjamin Stevens). In all, over twenty Congregational ministers can be identified as sympathetic to the Loyalist cause. Although a majority of the Loyalist ministers were Old Lights, no hard-and-fast connection between Old Light theology and Loyalism can be drawn since followers of Jonathan Edwards such as David Parsons of Amherst and John Hubbard of Northfield also defended Loyalist positions.

The sources of this Congregational Loyalism shared most of the characteristics of Loyalism within the other denominations. The Old Lights who embraced the Tory viewpoint often did so on the same grounds for which they denounced the revival — in neither religion nor government should mob enthusiasm be encouraged, disorder be fostered, or the untried freaks of fervid minds be substituted for the internal stability and decorum of the old order. What Clifford K. Shipton has written of the Congregational physician, William Brattle, could be applied equally to many of the other Congregational Loyalists in Massachusetts: "By the winter of 1773-1774 'Old Brattle,' like a majority of the men of his class, had decided that the political agitators and legal metaphysicians were driving the province into civil strife likely to produce more evil than good."[17]

Other, more explicitly religious motives also led to Congregational Loyalism. The Rev. Eli Forbes of Brookfield, a moderate New Light, thought that Christians, and particularly Christian ministers, should simply not be a part of a movement engendering strife and discord. With reference to the political strife, he wrote that the good Christian

will form no party schemes, or [enlist] under dividing

---

17. Clifford K. Shipton, *Sibley's Harvard Graduates* (vols. IV-XIV; Boston: Massachusetts Historical Society, 1933-1968), Vol. VII, 19.

names.... All such party attachments discover a carnal mind, and the want of the true spirit of Christianity. Nor will the good christian be discontented with the post in which the supreme Lord has fixed him, and break from his sphere like an eccentric body, to the disturbing or indangering the whole system.[18]

For the pains which he took in expressing such views, Forbes was harassed by the Patriots, who on one occasion hurled rocks at him and his wife and who later forced him to abandon his Brookfield pastorate.

Christian Loyalism during the Revolution was made up of many components. Christians who chose to resist the Patriotic tide did so as much for political, social, and cultural reasons as for explicitly religious ones. In this respect, however, they did not differ greatly from Christian Patriots who, more often than not, pledged allegiance to Patriotism for other than Christian motives. Neither Patriots nor Loyalists were reluctant to use religion as a means to enhance the appeal of political positions assumed for other than religious reasons. In so doing, Loyalists were as open as Patriots to the charge of prostituting Christianity before politics. Nevertheless, finer and higher motives also moved some of the Loyalists. Whatever one may say of their politics, those like Moses Dunbar, John Beach, and Eli Forbes maintained Christian convictions of high integrity, often in the face of the sharpest public hostility.

---

18. Eli Forbes, *Some Short Account ...* (Boston: Richard Draper & John Bayles, 1773), p. 135.

VI *The Pacifist Response*

To a considerable number of Christians in colonial America, questions concerning the morality of warfare itself were more important than questions about the merits of British Loyalism or American Patriotism. To these believers, talk of "winning" or "losing" the war evinced a failure to recognize that all who participated in warfare had *ipso facto* suffered irreparable loss through the destruction of spiritual as well as temporal possessions, through injuries to the soul as well as to life and limb. The witness of Christian pacifism has waxed and waned throughout the history of the United States. Recent questions about the morality of warfare have stimulated members of the "peace" churches to reappropriate their heritage. It has also led other Christians to examine once again the scriptural discussions of war and the state. The history of Christian pacifism during the American Revolution provides abundant material for serious reflection upon these topics.

The church bodies in Revolutionary America that maintained a pacifist stance included the Quakers, the Mennonites, the Church of the Brethren, and the Moravians. Mennonites were direct ecclesiastical descendants of the Anabaptists of the early sixteenth century. The Anabaptists, under such leaders as Menno Simons, for whom the Mennonites are named, sought a more radical reformation of Christian thought and practice than the "magisterial" reformers — Luther, Zwingli, Calvin, and Cranmer. In working out this more thorough reformation, Mennonites tried to implement a strict interpretation of biblical commands in the ecclesiastical, familial, vocational, social, and political affairs of daily life. To achieve these ends, Mennonites adopted views of the state and of the Christian's place in society which set them apart from the larger churches arising from the Reformation, with whom the Mennonites did however share central teachings concerning God's work in Christ.

The Society of Friends, known popularly as the Quakers, arose in England during the Puritan Revolution of the 1640's. Under the leadership of George Fox, Quakers held to the importance of an Inner Light of the living Christ as the key to true Christian knowledge, faith, and practice. Early Quaker teaching did not divorce this Inner Light from the commands of Scripture but saw it rather as an immediate experience confirming the truth of the Bible, producing salvation, and guiding the believer in daily living. Quakers shared the militant spirit of many of the sects of this period in English history even as they stressed the non-violent nature of the exertions required to bring about the victory of Christian goodness over evil.

The Moravians and the Church of the Brethren were products of the resurgence of German Pietism at the end of the seventeenth century. In 1722 a tiny remnant of the Bohemian Brethren, a Protestant-like sect with origins in fifteenth-century Czechoslovakia, was granted asylum on the estate of Nicholas Ludwig Count von Zinzendorf in Saxony. Over the next decade a great spiritual awakening brought about rapid growth for this group. Under the energetic leadership of Zinzendorf and others, the Moravians, as they were called with reference to their original emigration from Moravia, came to be characterized by an intense focus on the person and work of Christ and a great missionary energy. Although they did not lay great stress on doctrine, their missionary zeal led to rapid expansion in England, the colonies, and many other parts of the world. The Church of the Brethren arose at Schwarzenau, Germany, in 1708 as part of the general rejection of orthodox Lutheranism. As did the other Pietists, the Brethren manifested an earnest spirituality and an eagerness to follow the Bible's literal commands in daily life. Their distinctive nickname, Dunkers, came from the practice of trine baptism — that is, threefold, face-forward immersion.

By the time of the American Revolution all of these groups and a few smaller bodies such as the Schwenk-felders were represented by substantial numbers in America. The Quakers had been well represented in the New World even before William Penn founded Pennsylvania in 1681. With the establishment of Penn's "Holy Experiment," whose constitution proclaimed liberty of conscience for all Christians, Penn, a Friend himself, provided the Quakers with a hospitable American home. Although Quakers had been outstripped numerically in Pennsylvania by the time of the Revolution, they were still a dominant factor in the colony due to their entrenched social and economic positions and their relatively high population. Quakers were numerous also in New Jersey and Delaware, and they were present in Rhode Island, Massachusetts, and some of the southern colonies. Mennonites made up approximately one-thirtieth of Pennsylvania's population of 300,000 at the time of the Revolution. The preponderance of their adherents lived in southeast Pennsylvania with some representation in Delaware and western Maryland. The approximately 1,000 members of the Church of the Brethren were located mostly in Pennsylvania. Colonial Moravians were concentrated in North Carolina and east-central Pennsylvania.

These groups brought to the colonies a pacifist tradition that was deeply embedded in their theological heritage and that had been thoroughly tested by persecution in Europe. All of the groups acknowledged the biblical warrant for civil government, the necessity for police power in the state, and the inevitability of warfare among nations. They did not, however, feel that Christians should be involved in governmental processes when it was necessary to act in defiance of biblical standards or in opposition to the fundamental character of Christianity. As early as 1527 the first Anabaptist Confession of Faith had made a distinction between the necessary role of the state and the Christian's attitude toward violence:

> We are agreed as follows concerning the
> sword: The sword is ordained of God outside the per-
> fection of Christ. It punishes and puts to death the
> wicked, and guards and protects the good.... In the
> perfection of Christ, however, only the ban is used for
> a warning and for the excommunication of the one
> who has sinned, without putting the flesh to death.[1]

Slightly more than a hundred years later, the Mennonite Confession of Dort (1632) spelled out in greater detail the reasons for the renunciation of violence:

> Regarding revenge and resisting our ene-
> mies with the sword we believe and confess that the
> Lord Jesus Christ has forbidden His disciples and fol-
> lowers all retaliation and revenge, and has commanded
> them not to 'return evil for evil nor railing for railing,'
> but to 'put up the sword into the sheath' or, as the
> prophets foretold, 'beat them into ploughshares.'...
> From this we see that, following His exam-
> ple, life, and teaching, we cannot cause suffering, harm,
> or grief to any one, but we must seek the highest
> welfare and salvation of all men. We believe that, if
> necessity requires it, we should flee for the Lord's sake
> from one city or country to another and suffer 'the
> spoiling of our goods,' rather than cause suffering to
> any one. And if we are struck, we should turn the
> other cheek also, rather than retaliate or strike back.[2]

The Scripture passages quoted in this statement — Matthew
5:39, 44; I Peter 3:9; Isaiah 2:4; Micah 4:3; Matthew 10:23
— represent only a small portion of the biblical evidence
which members of the peace groups marshalled to defend
the Christian's disavowal of violence in public and private life.

The Quaker peace witness was based less on direct
scriptural precepts than on a sense of war's simple incon-
sistence with the Inner Light of Christ. The Friends' peace
position was formulated during a period of English history

---

1. In Peter Brock, *Pacifism in the United States: From the Colonial
Era to the First World War* (Princeton: Princeton University Press,
1968), p. 20.
2. In John Horsch, "An Historical Survey of the Position of the Mennonite Church on Nonresistance," *The Mennonite Quarterly Review,* I
(October, 1927), 4.

in which a wealth of religious and social novelties competed for popular support. The Quakers marked out their place in the spectrum in a declaration of January, 1661: against the most radical Christian sects of the Puritan Revolution, the Quakers renounced the sword as a means of bringing in the Kingdom of Christ. But against the main-line dissenters and the Church of England, Quakers also rejected violence as an instrument of ecclesiastical or national policy. In contrast to the Mennonites, Quakers did retain their conviction that a true believer could be both a ruler and a Christian. Indeed, Quakers exercised control of the Pennsylvania assembly until the time of the French and Indian War. From early in their history, however, they had clearly renounced the notion that warfare was compatible with Christianity or beneficial for society.

Because the Moravians and Dunkers had arisen in a Europe where simple survival was the overwhelming concern, their pacifist traditions were not as complex as those of the Quakers. These pietists had never had a real opportunity to exercise governmental authority in Europe. Inasmuch as their concern was for freedom to practice their beliefs without external distress, they resembled the Mennonites more than they resembled the Quakers. Pietistic pacifism was also based on the testimony of Scripture and on the general sense that warfare did not have a place in Christian life.

Peter Brock, author of the definitive history of early pacifism in the United States, has described the pacifists at the time of the American Revolution as groups with Old World beliefs encountering novel developments in the New World. There was nothing uniquely American in the pacifism of these groups:

> On the North American continent pacifism, the renunciation of war by the individual, represented at first a transplantation into these new and open territories of an attitude that had originated among religious groups in the European homeland. Antimilitarism and the refusal to participate personally in any warlike activity formed, as it were, part of the intel-

lectual baggage brought over the ocean by emigrants
from their midst.[3]

Although the pacifist positions of the Mennonites,
Quakers, Moravians, and Brethren were similar in form, some
differences did appear in their responses to the Revolution.
There is little wonder that the problems confronted by prominent English-speaking Quakers in Philadelphia would be different from those facing German-speaking Mennonites in
rural Pennsylvania. Pacifists maintained their testimony with
great consistency, but they were not untouched by the political currents of the time. As a result, even as they labored
to maintain their peace testimony, some leaned toward Loyalism and some toward Patriotism. In order to see the responses of Christian pacifists to the American Revolution
accurately, we must look briefly at the history of the major
peace sects before and during the conflict, then at the argument for pacifism as it came to expression during the period,
and finally at the few individuals from other denominations
who also testified against warfare at the time of the Revolution.

More than any of the peace denominations, Quakers bore the brunt of Patriotic attacks upon the pacifist
position. As late as 1755, Quakers had held a majority in
the Pennsylvania assembly. The grave crisis of 1755-1756
over participation in the French and Indian War resulted
in a fundamental shift in the Quaker attitude toward public
life. Prior to this time Quakers had participated quite successfully in the government of Pennsylvania. Quaker busi-
nessmen prospered and the Society of Friends had a very
secure place in the economic and social life of Philadelphia.
Under Quaker direction Pennsylvania as a whole had also
experienced great growth. The colony's tolerant administration encouraged immigration of the Mennonites and Moravians as well as of the Scotch-Irish Presbyterians and other
non-pacifists. Relations with the Indians on the Pennsylvania
frontier had been at times trying but were generally peaceful.
At mid-century, also, the spiritual health of the body was

---

3. *Pacifism in the United States,* p. 3.

being revived through the labors of John Woolman, Anthony Benezet, and others who sought to revitalize Quaker principles in the daily and corporate life of the Society.

Ironically, the very success of this revived spirituality led to the "exclusion" of Quakers from Pennsylvania political life when the ravages of war appeared ready to overwhelm the colony. As military pressure from the French and their Indian allies mounted on the frontier, monthly, quarterly, and yearly meetings of Friends exerted pressure of their own on the Quakers in the legislature to renounce military force and mandatory taxes for military purposes. The Scotch-Irish on the frontier complained bitterly about the lack of military protection. In their eyes, the Quakers had succumbed to a selfish love of ease and prosperity that was masquerading behind the pious mantle of religious scruples. In reality, however, the Quaker legislators were honestly facing the anomalous nature of their situation: as Quaker *legislators* they must see to the needs of the people, as *Quaker* legislators they are unable in good conscience to raise and outfit a militia. Pressure from the frontier grew along with increasing emphasis within Friend circles on the important place of pacifism in the Society's Christian testimony. Mediating Quakers inside and outside of government would have liked to appropriate money "for the king's use," funds which everyone knew were for defense against the French and their Indian allies. But this step was not active enough for the frontier and far too militaristic for the increasingly active defenders of a strictly Quaker style of life. In the end, when war was declared in 1756 and when harsh and violent measures against the Indians were urged by other colonial governments, six Friends resigned from the Pennsylvania legislature, and effective control of Pennsylvania's political life passed forever from Quaker hands. Many Friends hoped to regain political control once the French and Indian War was over, but the rising tide of pacifism within the Society and the increasingly raucous confrontations characterizing colonial political life after that war worked together to prevent further Quaker control. In fact, after the exclusion of 1755-1756, Quakers turned more and more to internal affairs, tended to exchange political for spiritual concerns, and grew much more interested in the internal quality of Quaker life than in its external impact on the world.

In the earliest stages of the Revolution, Quakers had little sympathy for Patriotism. Their pacifist principles made them extremely wary of any movement that used violent means to achieve its purposes. Not unnaturally, ends achieved by violence were equally suspect. In addition, since Quaker spirituality had never excluded an extensive study of Scripture, Quakers felt constrained to heed the precepts of Romans 13 and subject themselves to the ruling powers. They also reflected on their prosperity under British rule and wondered how they could possibly be better off under independent colonial government. As a rule, Quakers in England who knew the situation in British politics firsthand were much more sympathetic with the drive for American independence than were Friends in the colonies.

Four distinct issues faced the Quakers, and other pacifists as well, during the Revolution: (1) Should we serve in the militia? (2) Should we pay the commutation tax in lieu of military service? (3) Should we pay general taxes intended in part or whole for the prosecution of the war? (4) Should we swear the loyalty oaths demanded by the new independent provincial governments? The essential Quaker position was outlined in two documents issued by the Philadelphia Yearly Meeting in early 1775. The Philadelphia Meeting was not only the most articulately pacifistic group of Quakers in the colonies, but also the largest, wealthiest, and most influential. In a general letter to its members it cautioned them against entanglement in military affairs and urged them to adopt a nonresistant stance. Echoing the words of I Peter 2:17, this memorandum called on Quakers to remember "that to fear God, honor the king, and do good to all men, is an indispensable duty."[4] The second document was written as a public announcement of the Friends' position. This "Testimony of the People called Quakers" proclaimed forthrightly that the Society would "discountenance

---

4. *Ibid.*, p. 186.

and avoid every measure tending to excite disaffection to the King, as supreme magistrate, or to the legal authority of government." It went on to rue the fact that policies and strategies "have been pursued, which have involved the colonies in confusion, appear likely to produce violence and bloodshed, and threaten the subversion of . . . constitutional government, and of . . . liberty of conscience."[5]

These sentiments summarized the feelings of most colonial Quakers. Apart from a very small group of "Free Quakers" in Philadelphia who took up arms for the Patriot cause and a larger number of individual Friends who enlisted against the wishes of local meetings, Quakers approached the conflict with consistent commitment to their pacifist witness. There was, as a consequence, little disagreement or even discussion on the first issue, military service. No Quaker, while in good standing with his local meeting, could heed the call to arms or serve with the military forces of either side. The Quaker position on this point was forthright. It was, moreover, recognized and acknowledged by the new independent governments in America. The provincial assembly in Pennsylvania, the state in which by far the greatest number of colonial pacifists lived, dealt with the issue on June 30, 1775:

> The House, taking into consideration that many of the good people of this Province are conscientiously scrupulous of bearing arms, do hereby earnestly recommend to the Associators for the defense of the Country [local Patriots], and others, that they have a tender and brotherly regard towards this class of their fellow-subjects and countrymen; and to these conscientious people it is also recommended that they chearfully assist in proportion to their abilities, such Associators as cannot spend their time and substance in the public service without great injury to themselves and families.[6]

On July 18 of that same year the Continental Congress fol-

---

5. *Ibid.*, p. 187.
6. In "Preparing for Revolution," *Mennonite Historical Bulletin*, XXXV (July, 1974), 5.

lowed the Pennsylvania assembly's example. Its proclamation also combined solicitude for conscientious objectors with an appeal for their non-military help in the struggle against Great Britain:

> As there are some people, who, from religious principles, cannot bear arms in any case, this Congress intends no violence to their consciences, but earnestly recommends it to them to contribute liberally in this time of universal calamity to the relief of their distressed brethren in the several colonies and to do all other services to their oppressed country, which they can consistently with their religious principles.[7]

The real problems for Quakers and other pacifists in the colonies lay not in their exemption from military duty but in their failure to perform those tasks which the Patriot leaders thought it reasonable to demand in lieu of such service. Although most provincial assemblies did allow pacifists to object conscientiously to military service, they expected extra compensation in return for this privilege. The Pennsylvania assembly voted in November of 1778 to exempt conscientious objectors from the general draft, but also levied an annual fine of two and one-half pounds for this exemption. In Massachusetts a similar law of 1776 mandated a fine of not more than ten pounds or imprisonment of not more than two months for not answering the draft or not hiring a substitute. It seemed only fair to the Patriots to request these extra fees from those who refused active service for religious reasons.

The Society of Friends, however, saw the request in an altogether different light. A statement by the Philadelphia Yearly Meeting in September, 1776, stated the essential Quaker position:

> It is our judgment that such who make religious profession with us, and do either openly or by connivance, pay any fine, penalty, or tax, in lieu of their personal services for carrying on war . . . do

---

7. *Ibid.*, p. 6.

thereby violate our Christian testimony, and by so doing manifest that they are not in religious fellowship with us.[8]

Nothing could be plainer: paying for a war was the same as fighting in it. If it was wrong to kill, it could be no less wrong to pay someone else to kill. The logic of the Patriotic argument demanding compensation for release from military service was lost on the Quakers, who in the course of the war disciplined some 450 of their members for paying the commutative tax.

The logic of the Quakers, on the other hand, failed to impress the Patriots. For example, Tom Paine had nothing but sarcasm for the secretary of the Philadelphia Meeting, James Pemberton. In Paine's eyes the refusal to contribute monetarily to the war effort was little more than "crypto-Toryism." While recognizing the genuine religious sensibilities of a very few Quakers, Paine considered most of them to be as treacherous as the hated Jesuits: "O! ye fallen, cringing, priest-and-Pemberton-ridden people! . . . What more can we say of ye than that a religious Quaker is a valuable character, and a political Quaker a real Jesuit."[9]

With less concern than Paine for ideology and more for the practicalities of the situation, a "Committee of Philadelphia Patriots" petitioned the fall 1775 session of the Pennsylvania assembly against the pacifists. To this committee, Quakers and their ilk seemed unfriendly to the liberties of America and injurious to life in society. The committee contended that "these gentlemen want to withdraw their persons and their fortunes from the service of their country at a time when their country stands most in need of them."[10] Patriotic responses were not exhausted in vituperation and petition. Particularly when refusal to hire a substitute or

8. In *Pacifism in the United States,* p. 200.
9. Thomas Paine, *The American Crisis* (1777), in *The Writings of Thomas Paine,* ed. Moncure Daniel Conway (New York: G. P. Putnam's Sons, 1894), Vol. I, 208.
10. In William J. Bender, "Pacifism Among the Mennonites, Amish Mennonites and Schwenkfelders of Pennsylvania: Part II," *The Mennonite Quarterly Review,* I (October, 1927), 23.

pay a commutative fine was combined with refusal to pay war taxes or swear allegiance to the independent provinces, Patriotic reprisals moved from word to deed.

Quakers continued to pay taxes designated for highway repairs and the like, but they were loath to pay special levies for the war. Although there was some disagreement among the Quakers concerning the payment of "mixed" taxes — that is, general levies in which only a part was designed for military ends — sufficient Patriotic ire was incurred by the refusal to pay explicit war taxes that this slight ambiguity in the Quakers' own position did not materially effect the treatment they received from the Patriots. The Friends' stand on oaths followed the pattern of their general position. Viewing the oath as a sign of approval for independence that had been gained through violence, the Philadelphia Yearly Meeting said flatly in 1778: "We cannot be instrumental in setting up or pulling down any government." The North Carolina Yearly Meeting spoke out even more forthrightly in stating their objection to that province's loyalty oath: "The proposed affirmation approves of the present measures, which are carried on and supported by military force."[11]

For their pains in seeking to present a consistent pacifist testimony during the war, many Quakers spent at least some time in prison. As British pressure mounted on Philadelphia in early September, 1777, seventeen Philadelphia Quakers were arrested on charges of abetting the enemy. The charge was false, but the Quakers were held in detention for seven months. More commonly even than imprisonment, the Quakers lost property and land. Refusal to hire a substitute soldier or to pay a commutation fine often resulted in heavy and repeated fines. Judicial actions in distraint of goods or simple fines for the failure to pay war taxes cut deeply into the economic well-being of the members of the Society.

However much they resisted the bellicose spirit during the war, Quakers did not harden their hearts to the

---

11. Both quotations from *Pacifism in the United States*, p. 205.

temporal needs of their fellows. The Friends' Meeting for Suffering, a committee which sought to identify and alleviate incidents of persecution, was revived. More affluent Philadelphia Quakers sent funds to Massachusetts in 1774 to aid Friends and, later, all who suffered loss because of the hostilities. Even in its benevolence, however, the Society refused to be partisan. North Carolina Friends, for example, buried the dead and cared for the wounded of both sides after the battle at Guilford Courthouse on March 15, 1781.

With only a few exceptions, Quakers did not prosecute their pacifist viewpoint during the war. When pressed, Quakers would rehearse the traditional reasons for nonresistance and articulate a Christian justification for their actions. But in general the Quaker bent during the war was toward introspection instead of proselytization. The dream of regaining political power in Pennsylvania was no longer nourished. The need to solidify inner resources, to refine the character of the Society in accordance with its tradition, seemed more compelling than the drive to convince the world of its folly. A few Quakers whose pacifism shaded into Loyalism emigrated to Canada once the war's outcome became apparent. Most of the Quakers who remained thanked God for the strength to resist rampant militarism, besought divine aid in restoring normalcy in economic and social lives, and turned their hearts and minds ever more resolutely to the cultivation of the Inner Light.

The experience of other colonial pacifists did not differ significantly from that of the Quakers. Peter Brock describes the differences that did exist more in terms of tone than of substance:

> The religious pacifism of the Society of Friends, many of whom were city dwellers with a cosmopolitan culture, took a more militant, political character than that of the simple German-speaking farmers out in the rural counties, who wished to live withdrawn from all affairs of state provided the authorities did not ask them to contravene their religious conscience.[12]

---

12. *Ibid.,* p. 259.

Mennonites, whose history in the colonies was much shorter than that of the Quakers, nevertheless experienced only variations on the Quaker theme. On November 7, 1775, the basic Mennonite position was outlined in a declaration to the Pennsylvania assembly to which the Dunkers also affixed their signature. The petition first thanked God for his goodness in Christ and then praised the assembly for its declaration of June 30 exempting conscientious objectors from direct military service. The petition expressed the willingness of Mennonites and Brethren to do public good during this period, "it being our principle to feed the hungry and give the thirsty drink." Further: "We have dedicated ourselves to serve all men in everything that can be helpful to the preservation of men's lives, but we find no freedom in giving, or doing, or assisting in any thing by which men's lives are destroyed or hurt." The petitioners expressed their willingness, "according to Christ's command to Peter, to pay the tribute, that we may offend no man; and so we are willing to pay taxes, 'and to render unto Caesar those things that are Caesar's, and to God those things that are God's.' " The Mennonites and Brethren were "also willing to be subject to the higher powers, and to give in the manner Parliament directs us."[13] They were, in short, prepared to adjust to the realities of the Revolutionary situation insofar as their own principles allowed it.

The general lot of the Mennonites during the war was easier than that of the Quakers for two reasons. Concentrated in rural southeastern Pennsylvania, the nature and sincerity of the Mennonite peace testimony were often respected by the local authorities. Secondly, Mennonites were not quite as "hard-nosed" as the Quakers, for they were willing to pay the fine in lieu of military service and occasionally to serve as teamsters and wagonmasters when their goods were requisitioned by the Continental forces. There was also greater disagreement about the payment of war and mixed taxes. In fact, the first schism among the Mennonites in America (the Amish had split off in Europe) came in 1778

---

13. In "Preparing for Revolution," *Mennonite Historical Bulletin,* pp. 6-7.

as a result of disagreement over the wisdom of paying Pennsylvania's special war tax. Mennonites presented a more united front in refusing to swear loyalty oaths to the new governments. Severe reprisals often fell upon Mennonites for refusing to take the loyalty oaths, particularly in areas where isolated groups of Mennonites lived in the midst of ardent Patriots.

The refusal to take oaths of allegiance to the Continental Congress or the independent states grew from a fundamental uneasiness about several aspects of the Patriotic effort. Could Mennonites swear to uphold a governmental authority that had gained control through violent means? Could they in good faith renounce the oaths that had been sworn to the king of England when they had been allowed to emigrate from European persecution to the relative calm of the New World? And could they be at all sure that the new Patriotic governments, which did evince considerable instability at times, offered a better political arrangement than the English system, to which many pacifists owed the greatest degree of freedom they had ever experienced? When pacifists stated these questions publicly, Patriots were wont to rank them as Loyalists. In truth, it is more accurate to view most pacifists as real neutrals whose principles distanced them from the heat of the conflict and enabled them to perceive some of the moral ambiguities in the contending positions.

The practical difficulties experienced by Mennonites during the war arose out of their fidelity to their pacifist position. For refusing to pay a special war tax, the families of eleven Mennonite farmers in Upper Saucon, Pennsylvania, were subjected to severe retribution, as described in this contemporary account:

> All their said personal estate, even their beds, bedding, linen, Bibles and books, were taken from them and sold by the Sheriff to the amount of about forty thousand pounds. . . . From some of them all their provisions were taken and even not a morsel of bread left for their children. . . . As all their iron stoves were taken from them, though fastened to the freehold,

> they are deprived of every means of keeping their
> children warm in the approaching winter, especially at
> nights, being obliged to lie on the floor without any
> beds; . . . some of the men's wives were pregnant and
> near the time of deliverance, which makes their case
> the more distressing.[14]

When in 1783 three Mennonite farmers aided destitute British
prisoners escaping from the Lancaster, Pennsylvania, barracks
in order to put into practice their sect's stated intent of feed-
ing the hungry and giving the thirsty drink, they received
lengthy prison sentences and very heavy fines. Only through
an appeal to General Washington were these farmers, who
were not political Loyalists, able to have their prison terms
suspended and their fines reduced. The lot of most Mennonites was easier than that of many Quakers, but Mennonites too had ample opportunity to test the constancy
of their pacifist convictions during the American Revolution.

The experience of the Dunkers during the war
closely paralleled that of the Mennonites, with whom they
had joined in petitioning the Pennsylvania legislature. As a
smaller, geographically less cohesive group, a greater diversity
of responses to the war did arise, but in general the Dunkers
refused military service and the oath of allegiance while
differing among themselves on the desirability of paying
war-related taxes. The press of Christopher Saur, Jr., a
leading Dunker whose strong defense of pacifism had inspired
all of the peace groups in Pennsylvania, was destroyed by
local Patriots in 1778. The loss of this publishing arm,
accompanied by Saur's arrest for refusing to swear the test
oaths, was a severe blow to the Brethren. The violence of
reprisals against Saur led many members of the Church of
the Brethren to have some of the same doubts concerning
the morality of the Patriot cause that appeared among the
Mennonites.

The pacifism of the Moravians was not as deeply
rooted as that of the Anabaptists' heirs, nor did it stem from
as radical a pietism as the Dunkers'. Their closer contacts

---

14. In *Pacifism in the United States*, p. 263.

with European Lutheranism and, through Zinzendorf, with other Christian bodies in England and America made them somewhat less doctrinaire than the Quakers and somewhat less insular than the Mennonites or Dunkers. Consequently, their peace testimony was more complex than that of the other nonresistant bodies. With many Lutherans, the Moravians saw a greater distinction between the morality of civil and personal deeds. When a state armed itself for self-defense, the Christian could approve and even participate in that defense so long as the individual believer continued to renounce the use of force in personal affairs and worked to restrict the scope and use of governmental force. Following this line of thought, Moravians in Europe had paid war taxes and hired substitutes for military service, practices which were continued in America at the time of the Revolution.

The Moravians had shown their willingness to bear arms in self-defense during the French and Indian War. When enemy forces threatened the Moravian settlements at Bethlehem and Nazareth, Pennsylvania, the Moravian bishop August Gottlieb Spangenberg organized defenses in Bethlehem. Moravians in North Carolina also organized for self-defense later in that same conflict. Uncertainties did, however, continue to exist among the Moravians. Shortly before Spangenberg organized Bethlehem's defenses, ten Moravian settlers on the Mahoning River in Pennsylvania were massacred by Indians against whom they offered no resistance. Ironically, some twenty years later a group of Indians at Gnadenhuetten, Pennsylvania, who had been converted by Moravian missionaries would offer no resistance to Patriot militiamen who attacked and slaughtered them under the false impression that they were allies of the British.

The Moravian peace testimony, as these two incidents suggest, was not a mere formality. During the Revolution, John Ettwein, who had replaced Spangenberg as the Moravian leader, spoke out directly against the military violence by which Patriots hoped to end their dependence upon Great Britain. Ettwein's sentiments also reflected the widespread uncertainty among the pacifists concerning the powers to which they owed subjection:

> I would rather permit myself to be hacked to pieces than go to war, butcher people, rob people of their property or burn it down, swear that I owe no obedience to K[ing] G[eorge], that I desire to help maintain the independence of Pennsylvania, until and before the time and circumstances make it clear that God has severed America from England.[15]

The attraction of Loyalism was strong for Moravians who had found a secure haven in the New World as a result of British beneficence. J. Taylor Hamilton, the author of a standard denominational history, provides a clear picture of the Moravian situation at the time of the war:

> At the beginning of the contest the majority of the Brethren entertained conservative sentiments or refused to take sides. Non-combatants from conscientious convictions, they had no special interest in the principle "No taxation without representation"; *Magna Charta* had no deep significance to the great majority of them, of other than English birth; in their former homes *Habeas Corpus* was unknown; they had personally received no wrongs from government; rather in 1749 and since Britain had laid them under tribute of gratitude; and above all this they were citizens of the world in so true a sense and to such a degree through their readiness to follow their Master's commission, that it seemed to them of comparatively little moment under what civil authorities they lived.[16]

In spite of this predisposition, the Moravians came to express as much sympathy for the Patriot cause as was found in any of the pacifist groups. The ambivalence in the Moravian pacifist heritage provided scope for both moderate Patriotism and moderate Loyalism. Ettwein, for example, argued doggedly for a consistent and thorough nonresistant position, but still administered the sacraments to members of his congregation who had joined the Continental militia.

---

15. *Ibid.*, p. 306.
16. J. Taylor Hamilton, *A History of the Church known as the Moravian Church, or The Unitas Fratrum, or The Unity of the Brethren, during the eighteenth and nineteenth centuries* (Bethlehem, Pa.: Times Publishing Co., 1900), p. 251.

While Ettwein shared much of the Quaker animus against the war, he did not advocate the strict discipline by which the Society of Friends purged itself of all who deviated on the peace testimony. Moravians, in general, refused military service and the test oath, although they were less scrupulous about providing auxiliary services to the Continental forces. The General Hospital of the American army was quartered in Bethlehem on two different occasions, and from February, 1777, Bethlehem served as the chief depot of military stores for the American forces. The peace witness shone forth clearly from the Moravians during the Revolution, even if it was not as bright as the testimony of other nonresistant groups.

There was little subtlety to the pacifist argument during the American Revolution: participation of a Christian in warfare violated the express teachings of the Christian scriptures and the inherent character of the Christian life. The Quakers, as the most widely dispersed and most English of the pacifist groups, articulated the clearest reasons for Christian pacifism. A petition on behalf of three Massachusetts Quakers who had been imprisoned for refusing to hire substitutes for military service set out the biblical argument clearly. The petition to the Massachusetts General Court on behalf of these three declared:

> That they Profess themselves Friends & Cannot in Conscience take arms on Either Side in the Unnatural War Subsisting Between Great Britton and the American Colonies or in any other Warrs Whatever Because they think it is Contrary to the Precepts of Christ as Sett Forth in many Places in the New Testament and in no ways Lawful to Such as will Be the Disciples of Christ —
> first Christ['s] Command *that we should Love our Enemies* [Matthew 5:44] . . . But warr on the Contrary teacheth us to Hate & Destroy them. —
> 2 The apostle Saith . . . *that we Warr not after the Flesh & that we fight not with flesh & Blood* [II Corinthians 10:3; Ephesians 6:13]: But Outward warr is according to the flesh and against flesh & Blood for the shedding of the One & destroying of the other —

3 The apostle Saith . . . *that the Weapons
of Our Warfare are not Carnal but Spiritual* [II Co-
rinthians 10:4] But the Weapons of Outward Warr are
Carnal Such as Cannon, musketts, Spears, Swords &
of which there is no mention in the Armour Described
By Paul

4th Because that James Testafied *that Warrs
& Strifes Came from the Lust which was in the members of Carnal men* [James 4:1] But Christians those
that are Truly Saints have Crucified the Flesh with
the affection of Lusts therefore they Cannot Indulge
them by Waging Warr.

5th Christ says . . . that his Kingdom is not
of this world and therefore that his Servants Shall not
fight [John 18:36] Therefore Those that fight are not
his Disciples nor Servants and many other Passages
which are Omitted.[17]

The North Carolina Yearly Meeting of 1775 summarized what the Quaker peace testimony meant in the particular context of the American Revolution:

We Sincerely declare that it hath been our
Judgment and Principle from the first to this day, that
the Setting up and Putting down Kings and Government is God's Peculiar Prerogative for Causes best
Known to him self and that it is not our work and
Business to have any hand or Contrivance therein nor
to be Bussie Bodies in Matters above our Station much
less to Contrive the Ruin or Overturn of any of them;
but to Pray for the King and for the safety of our
Nation, and good of all men that we may live a
Peacable and Quiet Life in all Godliness and Hon-
esty under the Government which God is Pleased to
set over us and to yield a Chearful and active Submission to all such laws as do Interfere with our Consciences by Suffering under them without Resistance
or anything more than to Petition or Remonstrate
against them.[18]

17. In Arthur J. Mekeel, "New England Quakers and Military Service
in the American Revolution," in *Children of Light,* ed. Howard H.
Brinton (New York: Macmillan, 1938), pp. 258-259.
18. In Dorothy Gilbert Thorne, "North Carolina Friends and the Revolution," *The North Carolina Historical Review,* XXXVIII (July, 1961),
323-324.

In the actual course of the war, Quakers and other pacifists injected a moral consideration into many of the activities and circumstances of the period. Could a true believer patronize a colonial merchant who defrauded his government of a legal tax by smuggling tea into the colonies? Could a Christian accept or use the inflated Continental currency which did not live up to the promises printed on its face? Could a Christian pacifist deal in the spoils of war or accept payment in exchange for goods commandeered by military forces without compromising the peace witness? When pacifists were forced by conscience to go against the Patriotic grain and answer these questions in the negative, they testified once again to the intensity of their commitment to the demands of Christian truth.

The most forthright personal exponent of pacifism during the Revolution was Anthony Benezet, a Philadelphia Quaker. This ardent reformer not only directed public arguments against the morality of warfare, but in much the same manner as Samuel Hopkins or Jacob Green used the war as an occasion to press home other reforms in colonial life. A pamphlet published in 1778 indicates the breadth of his concern: *Serious Considerations On several Important Subjects; viz. On War and its Inconsistency with the Gospel. Observations on Slavery. And Remarks on the Nature and bad Effects of Spiritous Liquors.* Warfare and slavery, Benezet contended, proceeded from the evil desire to increase one's personal power and to control some other individual's person or property.

Benezet's argument was simple. He asks his reader merely to "consider the difference" between the ways of Christ and the ways of war:

> [Christ] positively enjoins us, to love our enemies, to bless them that curse us; to do good to those that hate us, and pray for them which despitefully use and persecute us. . . . The meek, the merciful and the pure in heart are by him pronounced to be the particular objects of divine regard. . . . On the other hand, War requires of its votaries that they kill, destroy, lay waste, and to the utmost of their power

distress and annoy, and in every way and manner deprive those they esteem their enemies of support and
comfort.

Benezet had a ready answer to anyone who would reply that
Christ was only speaking of the Christian's personal life and
not of his involvement in national military actions:

> What was at first the personal duties of
> single christians, when they were scattered over the
> face of the earth, . . . became afterwards national duties,
> when whole nations became christians. . . . For a chris-
> tian nation differs no otherwise from a christian person,
> than as the whole differs from one of the parts of
> which it essentially consists.[19]

If, as was generally accepted at the time, the colonies were
Christian entities because of their corporate allegiance to
Christianity, then they ought to exhibit in their corporate
affairs the same virtues which Christ had offered to cultivate
in the lives of his children. Benezet encapsulated the message which the pacifist groups desired to speak to the American Revolution in a short broadside also published in 1778:

> Let us, beloved Brethren, not forget our
> profession as Christians; nor the blessing promised by
> Christ to the Peacemakers, but let all sincerely address
> our common Father for ability to pray, not for the de-
> struction of our Enemies, who are still our Brethren,
> the Purchase of our blessed Redeemer's blood; but for
> an agreement with them.[20]

Benezet's appeal quite naturally found a ready response in the hearts of his fellow Quakers and in the minds
of other pacifists. What is far more striking is the extent
to which his sentiments would have found approbation within
other religious bodies which were not known for a pacifist
testimony. A significant, if not overwhelming, number of

19. Anthony Benezet, *Serious Considerations On several Important
Subjects . . .* (Philadelphia: Joseph Crukshank, 1778), pp. 2, 6.
20. Anthony Benezet, *Serious Reflections recommended to the Well-
disposed of any Religious Denomination . . .* (n.p.: n.p., 1778), p. 3.

American believers in the non-pacifist denominations did, however, share nonresistant sentiments to one degree or another. The mere recitation of these individuals and their positions will, like the references to Loyalist Presbyterians and Congregationalists, provide a fuller, more realistic picture of the relationship of Christianity and the American Revolution.

The patriarch of American Lutherans, Henry Melchior Muhlenberg, while not in the strict sense of the word a pacifist, harbored strong feelings about the general immorality of warfare. Like the Mennonites and the Moravians, Muhlenberg was grateful to the king of England for aid that had been rendered in bringing Lutherans out of the strife of Europe and into the spaciousness of America. Although one of Muhlenberg's sons served as a general in the Continental forces and another was active in the politics of the newly independent country, he could never bring himself to advocate anything but neutrality. Muhlenberg thought that the intense preoccupation with "independence" in the colonies expressed a desire to be free from God's laws as much as from political oppression. He thought the *vox populi* could as well be the *vox diaboli* as the *vox dei*. Contacts with drunk and roistering American soldiers did little to convince him of the moral superiority of the Patriot cause. In fact, the wanton pillaging and destruction proceeding from both British and American troops led him to doubt the possibility of moral sense on either side. By strict definition, Muhlenberg was a neutral rather than a pacifist, but his neutrality translated itself into a position very close to that of the moderate pacifists. His concern was for the fate of Christianity in this upsetting period. A leading historian of American Lutheranism, Theodore G. Tappert, has given a succinct summary of Muhlenberg's position in the war:

> His constant appeal was to Romans 13 as he urged all Lutherans, whether in territory controlled at the time by the British or in territory controlled by the Americans, 'to be obedient and loyal to the government which actually has power over us and protects us.' ... Muhlenberg held steadfastly to the view that it

was the duty of the church to preach the Gospel and
nothing but the Gospel in time of War or in time of
peace.[21]

Other American Protestants, from widely divergent
denominations, also regarded the war as immoral or as a
contradiction to real Christianity. The Rogerenes, a small
sect of breakaway Congregationalists centered in Mystic,
Connecticut, had been convinced by the Quaker testimony of
war's inappropriateness for the Christian and refused to take
part in the conflict. A very few New England Baptists, including elder Peleg Burroughs of Tiverton, Massachusetts,
saw all war as sinful and denounced the Revolution. Even
the Church of England had its pacifists. The Rev. John Sayre,
rector in Fairfield, Connecticut, expressed sympathy for the
Patriot cause but denounced the use of force in political
matters. Sayre avowed his affection for the colonies in no
uncertain terms: "America is my native country; all my connections are in it; I have enjoyed the liberty and plenty of
it . . . too long thankfully, not to be sensible of the value
of both, and to desire a continuance of them, if it be His
will." But because of his reading of the gospel and of Christ's
commands to do good to all men, he had to confess: "I
dare not . . . promise to take up and use any carnal arms
at all."[22]

Among the American-born Methodists, pacifist
sentiments were limited to the conviction that a minister
should not be involved in politics and warfare. Freeborn
Garrettson, a Maryland circuit rider, resisted severe Patriotic pressure to swear the oath of allegiance and was as a
consequence subjected to physical abuse from Patriotic gangs.
A Virginia Methodist, Jesse Lee, took a slightly different
stand. Although he agreed to do alternate service as a baggage handler for the Continental forces, he refused to be
responsible for killing his fellow human beings. Lee has left
a record of the internal debate which led to his rejection of
combat:

21. Theodore G. Tappert, "Henry Melchior Muhlenberg and the American Revolution," *Church History*, XI (September, 1942), 299, 301.
22. In *Pacifism in the United States*, p. 281.

> I weighed the matter over and over again, but my mind was settled; as a Christian and as a preacher of the gospel, I could not fight. I could not reconcile it to myself to bear arms, or to kill one of my fellow creatures; however, I determined to go, and trust in the Lord, and accordingly prepared for my journey.[23]

The pacifist witness during the Revolution deserves more attention than it has received. A significant minority of American Christians withstood many kinds of intense pressure in order to preserve the conviction that Christianity and the violent taking of life in military conflict were incompatible. That the nonresistant testimony of most pacifists during the Revolution resulted from their European heritage says less about the character of this witness than that it was maintained with integrity in the crises of the period. The testimony of Christian pacifism was neither the most prominent nor the most vocal of Christian responses to the American Revolution, but without an understanding of its nature and expression, the history of Christians in the American Revolution is incomplete.

---

23. *Ibid.,* p. 283.

VII *Thematic Summary*

The only conclusion that may be applied to all Christians in America during the Revolutionary period is that religious beliefs did not fall by the wayside when believers came face-to-face with the War for Independence. The many different Christian responses to the crisis make it impossible to offer all-inclusive summaries about Christians and the American Revolution, but carefully qualified answers can be given to general questions concerning the interrelationship of political, religious, and social thought during the period. The four questions which follow provide one means of summarizing at least some of the specific actions and ideas of believers during the Revolution:

    (1) What did the church do for the Revolution?
    (2) What did the church do to the Revolution?
    (3) What did the Revolution do to the church?
    (4) What did the Revolution do for the church?

    The first question, which brings attention to those favoring separation from Great Britain, may be answered on three levels. In a very limited sense, it is possible to conclude that Christian convictions lay at the root of the Revolutionary movement. It could be argued, in particular, that the full Puritan concept of the covenant — involving belief in divine sovereignty over the relationships between God and men and among men — provided a perspective on life in society without which Revolutionary thought could not have developed as it did. Because the presumption of God's special guidance and protection of the colonies was so strong in some

minds, it is not entirely inappropriate to view resistance to
Great Britain as a product of a particularly religious way
of looking at the world. H. Richard Niebuhr suggests the
extent to which this view of the Revolution may have validity:

> One may raise the question whether our
> common life could have been established . . . without the
> presence of the conviction that we live in a world that
> has the moral structure of a covenant and without the
> presence in it of men who have achieved responsible
> citizenship by exercising the kind of freedom that ap-
> pears in their taking upon themselves the obligations
> of truth-telling, of justice, of loyalty to one another,
> of indissoluble union.[1]

Recent scholarship on the widely shared political
ideology of the Revolution suggests, however, that religion
was more a fertile soil for the Revolution than its actual
root. The most important elements in the Patriotic perception of the conflict were derived from the distinctly political
values of the Whig world view. Concern for the uses and
abuses of power, fear of the corrupting influences of governmental authority, and fanatic devotion to the goddess
liberty bear the primary responsibility for the shape which
Revolutionary ideology assumed. Yet without the fertile soil
of the American religious tradition, without particularly Puritan preoccupations with original sin, the ongoing battle against
Satan, and the "liberty wherewith Christ hath made us free,"
Whig ideology would not have exerted such a powerful sway
in leading the thought and guiding the actions of the Patriots.
Similarities between the view of life in the world developed
by American Christianity and Real Whig conceptions of
political reality imported from England were responsible
for the sense of cosmic importance and the fervent religiosity
that permeated the Whig expressions of many Christians.

The nurture Christians provided to the Revolution extended beyond the fact that many believers saw history, human fallibility, and public virtue in much the same

---

1. H. Richard Niebuhr, "The Idea of the Covenant and American Democracy," *Church History*, XXIII (June, 1954), 134.

way as the Whigs did. It took but little effort to align the Puritan belief in a higher law ordained by God and standing in judgment over all men with the Whig world view in which the positive law of particular nations was subservient to natural human rights and the laws of reason. The fact that the heir of the Puritan discovered this higher law in the written pages of Holy Scripture did not lessen his natural bent toward the Whig conception of proper government. Whigs also labored to enshrine their higher law in words that would stand the test of time. The flurry of constitution writing in the individual provinces after 1776 and on a national scale in the late 1780's reflected a persistent Whig effort to specify in writing the higher principles of natural right and freedom which the unwritten British constitution failed adequately to protect. Bible-studying Puritans, of all people, knew how valuable it was to have the great principles of life recorded on paper for all to read, study, and apply.

In sum, while it is probably best not to view the ideology of the American Revolution as a product of explicit Christian conviction, the bond between Christian belief and Whig politics was strong in many minds. Without the fervent and dedicated allegiance of those believers who thought they saw Christian principles implicit in the Whig faith, the libertarianism which shaped resistance to Great Britain and guided the construction of a new nation would not have moved minds, hearts, and wills as it actually did.

The services which Christians rendered for the Revolution were by no means limited to the ethereal realms of political theory. John Wingate Thornton, a nineteenth-century historian, spoke more accurately than he knew in proclaiming: "To the Pulpit, the PURITAN PULPIT, we owe the moral force which won our Independence."[2] The week-in, week-out preaching ministry of the church did indeed play a very large role in the dissemination of the Whig political creed. The clergy were a highly educated and widely respected class throughout the colonies and particu-

---

2. John Wingate Thornton, *The Pulpit of the American Revolution* (Boston: Gould & Lincoln, 1860), p. xxxviii.

larly in New England. When ministers spoke, people listened. A modern student of the history of public speech in America has made this important observation about the impact of the minister's public ministry on political thought: "Year after year the preacher reaffirmed from his high pulpit that both revelation and reason pointed to a single set of principles which outlined the best form of government."[3] We have seen that by no means did all colonial ministers share the Whig point of view, but enough of them did and enough of them were ready to bring politics openly into their pulpits that the widest possible airing of the Patriotic argument was ensured.

An impressive array of festal occasions provided the Whig ministers with opportunities beyond the weekly Sunday sermon in which to discuss scriptural principles of human government and to apply these principles to the current scene. The yearly election sermons in Connecticut and Massachusetts offered an extraordinary occasion for a learned minister to instruct the assembled legislatures, the governor, and a healthy proportion of the colony's clergy in those principles of government that were pleasing to God. Since these election preachers were almost always Whigs, their sermons tended to tie the knot between libertarian and Christian points of view even more securely. Special days of fasting or thanksgiving proclaimed by provincial legislatures in each of the colonies as well as by the Continental Congress itself allowed the ministers to reflect publicly upon God's dealings with the colonies in military, diplomatic, and civil affairs. Divergent points of view were heard in these sermons, and the exact application of divine truth to the contemporary situation would vary as the sermon was preached by a Charles Chauncy, Ezra Stiles, Jacob Green, George Duffield, Moses Mather, or John Witherspoon. But the assumptions undergirding the enterprise were nearly always the same: God *did* have a perfect plan which could be implemented in colonial society; to follow that plan would

---

3. Harry P. Kerr, "The Election Sermon: Primer for Revolutionaries," *Speech Monographs*, XXIX (March, 1962), 18.

ensure victory over personal sin, corporate corruption, and the British.

Christians rendered signal service to the Revolution. Religious thought invigorated the political ideology which demanded a break with Great Britain. The institutions and traditional exercises of Christianity provided a weighty sanction for the Patriotic message and a ready conduit for its dissemination. Allegiance to Patriotism and its Whig ideology was not universal among colonial Christians, but it was widespread and compelling. No study of the foundation and exposition of Revolutionary thought can omit it and present a true picture of the American Revolution.

Answers to the second question — what did the church do to the Revolution? — will have to be qualified in even more ways than answers to the first. Many believers were merely swept along in the Patriotic surge without exerting significant influence on the ultimate shape of the movement. Other Christians, however, interacted energetically with Revolutionary ideology to heighten its impact, or to broaden its range of application, or to reform its thrust by applying higher standards to it. That is, some Christians acted to make the Revolution a holy crusade, some sought to extend its influence over social as well as political matters, and some tried to give it a conscience.

Shortly after the promulgation of the Declaration of Independence, Ezra Stiles set down his feelings concerning the conflict with Great Britain. The process by which a political and military struggle between the colonies and their mother country was being transformed into a divinely inspired mission for truth and righteousness had already reached an advanced state in his thinking:

> God has caused us to suffer in a most glorious Cause, a Cause in which the Interest of the Redeemer's Kingdom is deeply involved.... Let our Hosts go forth in the Name of the Lord. In our unquestionably righteous Cause: ... till our Enemies shall be discomfited, and our Country and the Church of

God, gloriously delivered. And then let him have all
the Glory.[4]

The colonists who felt that God held the American provinces
in the special sun of his esteem almost invariably perceived
the military struggle as a spiritual battle. If as far back as
the Stamp Act crisis a Connecticut election preacher could
pray in one breath for "cordial friends to *Christ and his
Church, and patriots to the republick,*"[5] it is little wonder
that the Revolution itself encouraged an even stronger linking of the colonial cause and the special concerns of the
Lord. Once God had been enlisted on the colonial side, the
millennial fervor which had never been far from the heart
of American Puritanism invigorated the civil strife of the
Revolutionary era with a new energy. This "civil millennialism," in Nathan O. Hatch's perceptive description, "advanced freedom as the cause of God, defined the primary
enemy as the antichrist of civil oppression rather than that
of formal religion, [and] traced the myths of its past through
political developments rather than through the vital religion
of the forefathers. . . ."[6] The energetically entertained conviction that God favored the colonial cause bestowed upon
the Revolution something of the character of a medieval
crusade. If "God wills it" — the phrase emblazoned on the
crusaders' banners in the middle ages — also applied to the
effort to throw off British rule, the fight for God *and* country could be waged without mental or religious reservation.

While some believers used religion to heighten
the emotive impact of Revolutionary ideology, others em-
ployed it in an effort to broaden the scope of the conflict.
In Chapter Four we noted the attack by Isaac Backus, Israel
Holly, and other New England dissenters against the formal

---

4. *The Literary Diary of Ezra Stiles,* ed. Franklin Bowditch Dexter
(New York: Charles Scribner's Sons, 1901), Vol. II, 48-49. I have expanded the contractions which Stiles used here.
5. In Oscar Zeichner, *Connecticut's Years of Controversy, 1750-1776*
(Chapel Hill: University of North Carolina Press, 1949), p. 74.
6. Nathan O. Hatch, "The Origins of Civil Millennialism in America:
New England Clergymen, War with France, and the Revolution," *William and Mary Quarterly,* 3rd ser., XXXI (July, 1974), 429.

establishment of religion in that region. In the southern colonies during the war years similar appeals for an end to an officially established religion were made by dissenters from Anglicanism. Although different denominations held legal status as the established church in New England and the South, the nature of the case for disestablishment and the force with which it was argued were similar in both regions. Baptists in New England and Presbyterians in Virginia thought the legislated requirement to acknowledge a legal establishment of religion constituted a mortal impediment to proper Christian life. The common political arguments of the Revolutionary period took on ecclesiological as well as political significance. Dissenting Christians argued that talk of "freedom" must not be limited to the political relations between Great Britain and the colonies, but must be applied as well to the other aspects of life within the colonies, including the establishment of religion.

The Christian attack on slavery was also able to benefit from the elaborately constructed political arguments turned against Great Britain. Believers stood in the forefront of those who contended that "life, liberty, and the pursuit of happiness" must be the goals not only for American society in general but for each individual — black or white — in that society. The New England Congregationalists Samuel Hopkins and Levi Hart, the New Jersey Presbyterian Jacob Green, and the Philadelphia Quaker Anthony Benezet labored to show Americans that arguments against the tyranny and corruption of Parliament could not be artificially restrained from application to Negro servitude in the colonies.

Some historians have also felt that a religious impetus lay behind the movement from the highly structured, elitist, stratified colonial society to a democratic, egalitarian United States. Viewed in this way the American Revolution — that is, the War for Independence from Great Britain — was merely one phase in the true American revolution that changed the society imported from the Old World and characterized by inequality into a society aspiring to equality and adapting itself to the limitless horizons of the New World.

William G. McLoughlin, in his thorough studies of the Baptists of New England in the eighteenth century, has argued that for the Baptists, "to end spiritual tyranny so that the light of divine truth might shine clearly into each darkened soul called for a social and political revolution." The Baptists, McLoughlin concludes, were thoroughly egalitarian, and the thrust of their beliefs and practices from the Great Awakening onward worked for "the breakdown of the static, aristocratic, class-stratified, and carefully controlled social order of the old colonial society."[7] From this point of view, the sources of the colonial unrest concerning Great Britain's imperial policies can be traced to religious developments which had made the imposition of Old World concepts of order, legality, and hierarchy obsolete. Other historians have questioned the exact character of this so-called "revolution at home" or whether religion actually did inspire a social reorganization in the colonies. If these latter students of the period are correct and Christianity did not exert a fundamental influence on the construction of a new and democratic American mind during the American Revolution, it does not alter the fact that specific Christians during the 1770's did try to broaden the impact of Revolutionary thought, especially by applying Revolutionary ideology to the struggle to free churches from legal establishments and to free slaves from bondage.

Some of the very individuals who sought to broaden the scope of Revolutionary thought also played important roles in giving the American Revolution a conscience. While the Christian religion heightened the impact of Patriotism for many Christians, it exercised a restraining and chastening effect for others. Even John Witherspoon and Charles Chauncy, who supported the Patriot cause so unreservedly, did upon occasion remind their listeners of the need to repent of their own sins. What was true in part for these Patriot champions was true in greater measure for those like Israel Holly and Samuel Hopkins who saw more clearly that the manifest wickedness of the British could not take

---

7. William G. McLoughlin, *Isaac Backus and the American Pietistic Tradition*, pp. 2, 231.

away the need for repentance in the colonies. Those such as the Anglican Jonathan Boucher or the Moravian John Ettwein who simply failed to recognize that British "evil" justified the frenzied colonial response had an even stronger motive to urge repentance upon Americans. Much of the effort to instill into the Revolutionary atmosphere a moral sense which transcended the political debate was doubtlessly in vain. Equally without doubt, however, is the conclusion that one of the most significant features of Christian behavior during the Revolutionary period was the extent to which certain believers tried to prick the conscience of Americans. The moral sensibilities of those who made this effort were not exhausted by the categories of political expediency or totally captured by the conspiratorial mentality of the age but were, by contrast, faithful in allegiance to the law of Christ.

Our third summarizing question — what did the American Revolution do to the church? — can be answered on a number of different levels: ecclesiastical, sociological, and ethical. The most obvious response to this question is that the Revolution brought about the institutional liberation of churches from the official controls of government. Although the first amendment to the United States Constitution was a product of deliberations in the late 1780's, the principle which it embodied — "Congress shall make no law respecting an establishment of religion, or prohibiting the free exercise thereof" — had triumphed during the Revolutionary period. The famous Virginia Statute of Religious Liberty (1786) gave a definitive expression to the new view on the church-state relationship: official governmental control of the internal life of churches was a thing of the past. Connecticut and Massachusetts retained vestiges of their Congregational establishments into the nineteenth century, but even in these strongholds of ecclesiastical conservatism the scales tipped rapidly in favor of religious freedom.

The eighteenth-century rationale for doing away with established churches was two-fold. On the one hand, heirs of the colonial Great Awakening argued that true heart religion was incompatible with the legal coercion implicit in formal establishments. On the other hand, rationalistically inclined political leaders, particularly in Virginia, doubted the wisdom, or even the possibility, of forcing the varied human conceptions of Divinity into a single mold. Within the Revolutionary situation, these pietistic and rationalistic forces made common cause against the various legal restraints which circumscribed religious life in the different colonies. Complaints against the Church of England's ecclesiastical tyranny rang hollow where they were not matched by protests against indigenous ecclesiastical oppression. At first it was the Baptists in New England and the Presbyterians in Virginia who pointed out this fundamental inconsistency. Their arguments supported the labors of the rationalists who, for different reasons, had the same ends in view. Without the War for Independence, liberation from official governmental controls in religious affairs would probably have been a gradual phenomenon in American history; with the Revolution, however, ecclesiastical freedom became a highly visible symbol of the nature of the freedoms for which the Patriots had wagered their lives, fortunes, and sacred honor.

The sociological impact of the Revolution upon the church was not as favorable as its ecclesiastical influence. The churches were officially freed from governmental tampering, but they were also displaced from their earlier prominence as the sources of intellectual leadership for the colonies. Edmund S. Morgan has described the situation in American intellectual life like this:

> In 1740 America's leading intellectuals were clergymen and thought about theology; in 1790 they were statesmen and thought about politics.... one may properly consider the American Revolution ... to mean the substitution of political for clerical leadership and of politics for religion as the most challenging area of human thought and endeavor.[8]

In the mid-eighteenth century the ideas of Edwards, Chauncy, Samuel Davies, and other colonial ministers of varied points

---

8. Edmund S. Morgan, "The American Revolution Considered as an Intellectual Movement," in *Paths of American Thought,* ed. Arthur M. Schlesinger, Jr., and Morton White (Boston: Houghton Mifflin, 1963), p. 11.

of view were the centers of the most intense intellectual activity in the colonies. By 1800 it was John Adams, James Madison, Thomas Jefferson, and national political leaders who set the tone for American intellectual life. By the end of the eighteenth century, and largely as a result of the Revolution, the church no longer determined the agenda for intellectual life in the colonies.

The role of the Revolution in bringing this about is evident when one considers the relative impact of political and religious ideas upon Christians during that conflict. Ministers and other Christian leaders were powerless to prevent politics from becoming the all-consuming focus of colonial attention. It may seem incomprehensible to modern Americans that religious "news" could ever have seemed more important than political and economic affairs, but such was the case in the American colonies until the mid-eighteenth century. Throughout colonial history and most spectacularly during the Great Awakening, the religious perspective dominated the intellectual and cultural interests of Americans. After the War for Independence this was no longer the case. Affairs of state, internal political divisions, and expositions of political views assumed the place in American society that the ongoing history of redemption, ecclesiastical divisions, and expositions of theological views had once held.

The relative loss of influence by the church is indicated also by the powerlessness of religious leaders to alter the nature of the political thought dominating the Revolutionary era. Efforts by Samuel Hopkins or Anthony Benezet to apply Christian standards to the outworking of Whig ideology and to reform the Revolutionary movement along religious lines were not overly successful. Much more typical, in fact, were the labors of John Witherspoon or Thomas Chandler, who used Christianity as an *ex post facto* justification for political positions already advocated for other than religious reasons. The shift in priorities was not so dramatic that Witherspoon or Chandler held their religious convictions hypocritically, but it was of sufficient magnitude that religious perspectives played a distinctly less important role in political matters in 1776 than had been the case in

1676. It is not that religion was no longer important in the colonies during the Revolution. It is rather that political ideology had assumed religion's role as the fashioner of the most creative ideas in America. From being the queen of sciences, theology was well on the way to becoming the hand-maiden of politics.

Finally, in addressing the question of what the Revolution did to the church, it is necessary to consider whether Christian integrity was not swamped in the tide of Revolutionary feeling. From a twentieth-century perspective it appears as if all sense of perspective was lost, particularly where no doubts were countenanced about the righteousness of the Patriot cause. Where presbyteries could exclude ministers from fellowship because of failure to evince ardent Patriotism, where the "cause of America" could be described repeatedly and with limitless variation as "the cause of Christ," and where the colonists so blithely saw themselves standing in the place of Israel as God's chosen people, the question must arise whether the Revolution did not occasion a momentary moral collapse in the churches. Those ministers and lay believers who allowed the supposed justice of the Patriot cause and displays of Patriotic devotion to replace standards of divine justice and the fruit of the Spirit as the controlling determinants of thought and behavior be-trayed basic principles of the Christian faith — that abso-lute loyalty belongs only to God, and that unwarranted self-righteouness is as evil as open and scandalous sin.

The fourth question — what did the Revolution do for the church? — invites some repetition. Legal freedom in religious matters, for example, could be seen as something done for the church as much as to the church. In at least two areas, however, the Revolution did perform distinct services for Christianity in America. In the first instance, it released colonial Christians from fear of the Church of England. Whether or not the intense preoccupation with ecclesiastical tyranny before the war was justified, it was an active ingredient in the explosive mixture of mistrust and suspicion hastening the conflict. After the war this fear was removed, and its removal benefited all of the churches in the colonies. Members of the Protestant Episcopal Church in America were freed from the taint of British imperial policies; they could now take action to strengthen their internal structure and external outreach without having to worry about the political malevolence of non-Anglicans in the colonies. The other Protestant bodies in America benefited from the opening of the southern states to evangelism and proselytization. In this region as well as in the newly opened western lands, Baptists and Methodists were particularly responsive to the opportunities signaled by the end of legal domination by the Church of England. Even if the Anglican threat had been more psychological than actual, its removal was conducive to a freer religious atmosphere in America.

Secondly and with more particular reference to the period of the War for Independence, the struggles and hardships of the period provided opportunities for repentance and reform. Almost none of the ardent Patriots was so thoughtless as to totally neglect the gospel imperatives. Some heirs of the Puritans, as we have noted at length, labored long and diligently to show where the colonists themselves fell short of God's standards. The peace churches were encouraged to rethink and reapply their pacifist standards under the pressure exerted by the militaristic environment in America. And Christians loyal to Great Britain were also able to "improve" their trying situation in spiritually profitable ways. Appeals for repentance and reform were not the most prominent features in the politico-religious landscape of Revolutionary America where the breath-taking amalgamation of libertarianism and Christianity or the courageous resistance exhibited by Christians with minority viewpoints were of more obvious interest. But underneath the thunder and the gore, the rapturous Patriotism and the resolute nay-saying, less spectacular (but no less important) responses to the gospel were taking place. If these do not loom large in the picture of religion in the American Revolution, they nevertheless did exist and deserve acknowledgment in historical reconstructions of the period.

The four questions providing the structure for

this chapter do not admit of simple answers. Differing degrees of generalization are appropriate in answering them, but no comprehensive responses adequately describe the thoughts and actions of all Christians in all places during the Revolution. Given the many different ways in which Christians reacted to the War for Independence, it is only fitting that summary questions reveal the diversity of Christian behavior within the Revolutionary situation.

VIII The American Revolution and the Religious History of the United States

*As the course of American history in the nine-*teenth and twentieth centuries owes its direction to more than the events occurring during the War for Independence, so American religious history owes its shape to influences other than Christian activities during this period alone. Successive waves of immigrants have brought religious patterns from European and Asian homelands that have had a far-reaching effect on the general nature of religious life in the United States. The wide open spaces of the continent's heart-land and the loosely organized cultural institutions which characterized large sections of the country into the twentieth century also exerted a telling influence on the development of religion in America. And the growth of technology and urbanization since the last century has presented church-men with novel problems for which solutions from the past are not adequate. Recognizing the importance of these and other factors does not, however, detract from the decisive role which late eighteenth-century American history played in the development of religious life in the United States. Nor does it lessen the impact which the Revolutionary mixture of politics and religion has had on the public history of the country. While the ideas and actions of Christians at the time of the American Revolution did not lock succeeding generations into the patterns of the Revolutionary generation, they did exert a profound influence on the subsequent religious life of the independent United States.

In the first and most important place, Christians in America continued to assume that God had singled out the American nation for special privileges and responsibilities. Even before the Revolution, the assumption that God favored the English nation and its American colonies was widespread, but this conviction was reforged with new intensity in the violent crucible of events that saw the United States break its ties with the mother country. The growing belief that Europe had entered a period of decadence led to a corresponding conviction that God's children were concentrated particularly in America. When the events of the Revolution seemed to bear out this assumption, when it became clear, in Moses Mather's words, "that it is God that fighteth for us,"[1] belief in America's special place in God's esteem took even firmer hold on the masses of Christian Americans. Against all odds, God had prospered the valiant efforts of his colonial children as they struggled to throw off the immoral tyranny of their despotic masters.

The elaborate system of covenantal thought which had undergirded earlier expressions concerning God's care for the colonies was largely abandoned during the second half of the eighteenth century, but the essential dogma of the covenantal system — that the colonies stood in a special relationship to God — survived as an article of faith throughout the denominational spectrum. By 1800 the assertion that God dealt with the United States in a unique way was a commonplace. In New England, for example, the opponents and the adherents of the theological system developed by Jonathan Edwards both accepted this conviction. An anti-Edwardsean, Joseph Lathrop of West Springfield, Massachusetts, spoke in 1795 of "the blessings ... with which a gracious providence has distinguished our happy lot." Another opponent of Edwards' thought, Moses Hemmenway of Wells, Maine, used the public observance of George Washington's death as an occasion to remind his listeners that

1. Moses Mather, *Election Sermon* (New London: Timothy Green, 1781), p. 16.

God was still dealing with America by means of special chastisements and rewards.[2] On the other side of the theological fence, the Edwardsean Cyprian Strong of Chatham, Connecticut, could proclaim in 1799 that "we enjoy privileges and blessings, which are not realized by any other nation on earth." And in 1801 the incumbent at Edwards' old preaching station in Stockbridge, Massachusetts, Stephen West, could pray "that Zion [i.e., America] may soon hear the voice, *Arise, shine, for thy light is come.*"[3]

This conviction that God dealt singularly with America continued to hold sway into the nineteenth and twentieth centuries. The final disestablishment of Congregationalism during the first third of the nineteenth century and the irrevocable spread of denominationalism throughout America during the same period meant that the way in which God's special relationship with America was understood lacked the sharp focus it had had in Puritan New England. Nevertheless, the practice of America's "civil religion" continued to flourish, as was manifest particularly in that great outburst of Christian evangelism and social involvement marking the entire first half of the nineteenth century. To all who would listen in the great metropolises and in tiny prairie outposts, revivalists such as Charles G. Finney proclaimed the need for Christian conversion. Christian social reformers such as Lyman Beecher organized countless service agencies to encourage Christian practice in the country. Abolition, temperance, benevolence to orphans, sailors, and prostitutes, and societies to support missions, Sunday schools, and Christian literature were merely a fraction of the enterprises spawned in this era. Beneath the torrents of activity lay the conviction that had gained new consciousness during the Revolution — America's duty was to respond to the singular blessings which God had bestowed upon the nation. Al-

2. Joseph Lathrop, *National Happiness...* (Springfield, Mass.: J. W. Hooker & F. Stebbins, 1795), p. 15; Moses Hemmenway, *A Discourse Occasioned by the Lamented Death of General George Washington* (Portsmouth, N.H.: Charles Peirce, 1800), p. 12.
3. Cyprian Strong, *The Kingdom is the Lord's...* (Hartford: Hudson & Goodwin, 1799), p. 45; Stephen West, *Sermon, delivered on the Public Fast...* (Stockbridge, Mass.: Heman Willard, 1801), p. 15.

though external circumstances were altered significantly during the nineteenth century and although the particular correlations of theological and socio-political attitudes characterizing the Revolutionary age broke down in that same period, patterns of response from that earlier day continued to define the ways in which Christians viewed the relationship of religion and society.

As in the Revolution, a crusading zeal continued to mark those believers who sought the social changes which they felt Christian principles demanded. The Christian Patriotism of John Devotion shared with the abolitionism of Samuel Hopkins an urgent fervency which tended to equate the attainment of a particular goal in society with the triumph of Christian righteousness. Christian reformers in later American history continued to approach social problems in this same way. The reforms for which Christians have struggled have been diverse — abolition, prohibition, the destruction of godless foreign foes, an end to American involvement in foreign wars — but the presupposition underlying the various campaigns has been the same: when this reform is accomplished, America will have fulfilled its destiny as a uniquely Christian nation. The sources of this crusading zeal in the history of American Christianity are many, but not the least of them was the example of militant Christian advocacy during the American War for Independence.

Millennial overtones have also persisted in the course of America's history, due at least in part to the thorough millennialism that marked such a large part of the religious reaction to the Revolution. The way in which America's ideals of freedom and justice have been championed in public discourse has encouraged the idea that perfect freedom and perfect justice might be obtainable through the concentrated efforts of those upon whom God has already bestowed a foretaste of these blessings. During the Revolution, Christians felt that a successful completion of the war might be the prelude to the visible appearance of the Kingdom of God on earth. In later American history the millennial vision lost its sharp theological definition, but nevertheless lived on. Whether paternalistically in concern for our little brown brothers (President William McKinley), idealistically in the struggle to make the world safe for democracy (Woodrow Wilson), or with utopian fervor in the pledge to fight any foe in the defense of freedom (John F. Kennedy), Americans have taken seriously the founding fathers' assertion that the United States represented a *novus ordo seclorum* (a new order for the ages). Even as the objects of reforming zeal have changed throughout American history, so has the precise makeup of America's millennial vision. Without an understanding of the intense millennialism of the Revolutionary period, however, later American ideals for its own character and its role in the world can never be fully understood.

In sum, the Revolutionary period provided an opportunity for a modified Puritan synthesis to retain its viability in America. No longer adhering to the express tenets of Puritanism, American Christians after the Revolution nevertheless worked to maintain personal religion and a comprehensive Christian community. At least partially as a result of the war, American society in general replaced the church as the locus of communal Christian values. Because it was so obvious during the Revolution that God was concerned with the entirety of the American experience instead of merely ecclesiastical expressions, the transition from Puritan Christianity to American Christianity was made smoothly. Since God had so manifestly blessed the national enterprise during the war, the deduction could be made that God took a special interest in the nation as such. Americans who have had only nominal contact with Christian churches, or perhaps none at all, have been only slightly less eager to adopt the assumptions concerning a unique salvific role for the United States in the history of the world. An accounting of the religious and political relationship at the time of the American Revolution helps to explain how the concept of a Christian America came to be shared so widely both by sincere believers and the nominally religious in the United States.

The discussion in this chapter has been mainly concerned with the effects which the admixture of religious and political ideology during the Revolution wrought upon public life in the United States. The Revolution was no less important in shaping the internal life of American churches. During the war, religion lent its weighty support to political and social values emanating from nonreligious sources. This same pattern continued after the end of the conflict. Where colonial Christians in 1700 derived much of their world view from strictly theological sources, American Christians in 1800 absorbed much of their basic outlook on life from the surrounding culture. The shift that we have noted in intellectual leadership from ministers to statesmen entailed a definite alteration in the relationship of Christianity and culture in America. In 1700 religion had been an "exporter" of ideas and behavior patterns to American society; by 1800 it was an "importer." The ideas by which men lived, which dictated the allotment of their time and energy, which shaped the way they approached conflicts in society, and from which they developed their systems of values, came increasingly from nonreligious sources as the eighteenth century wore on. While Christians in early colonial America were by no means immune to influences from secular sources, these influences were outnumbered and outweighed by the products of religious thought and experience. By contrast, although believers during the early history of the United States maintained active religious lives, the major practical influences shaping their perspective on life were no longer the products of religious thought. It is not that religious activity diminished in late eighteenth- and early nineteenth-century America, but rather that the nature of that religious activity came more and more to be influenced by ideas from outside the church. Jonathan Edwards, the last American religious thinker whose ideas have had a formative effect upon American culture, died in 1758. The most important influences upon the American mind after Edwards came from men like Jefferson, Hamilton, and Madison who were concerned with public affairs and whose debt to religious thought was minimal.

The practical upshot of this development was that the thought and activity of the American churches tended to follow the thought and activity of the American nation. The ideals which had been fought for in the Revolution or which lay embedded in the arguments for independence — the ideals enshrined in the great national documents produced from 1776 to 1789 — came also to be the ideals of the churches. The convictions that men had rights by nature, that the pursuit of personal happiness was one of these unalienable rights, that all men were essentially equal, that personal freedom was necessary for social well-being, and that a collective "people" had it within their power to establish justice or secure the blessings of liberty to themselves and their posterity became the dogmas not merely of the new nation but also of its churches. The fact that these national ideals resembled many of the ideals of earlier American Christianity eased the process by which the churches assimilated the American political creed.

One of the most obvious indications that American Christians were following the thinking arising out of the Revolution was the acceptance of voluntaristic denominations as the standard for ecclesiastical organization. To be sure, other important factors besides the Whig ideology of the Revolution went into the formation of the American denominational system. The new United States government lacked the means or the will to control the religious lives of its people, and the presence of so many different religious groups in the new country made some system of mutual toleration and respect a necessity. But Whig ideology also played a part in sanctioning a state of affairs which natural conditions had brought about. From the Revolution, Americans took strong ideas about the sanctity of natural rights and the dangers of governmental interference in personal affairs. What could be more natural than the right to construct a relationship with God on one's own terms? In keeping with the implications of this concept of freedom, American Christians came gradually to contend that no denomination could be inherently favored by law and that no law could interfere in the peaceable internal functions of the churches. This type of thinking strikes the twentieth-century American as commonplace, but in the eighteenth century, where the legal establishment of religion was the rule throughout the western world, American practice was truly innovative.

There were, moreover, influences from Whig ideology in the construction of the American denominational system. Political Whigs took it for granted that the people were capable of constructing their own political and social institutions. The idea of the social contract which influenced so much of eighteenth-century political theory presupposed this capacity as one of its unquestioned axioms. Although they were departing radically from earlier ecclesiastical patterns, American Christians under the influence of Whig thought also acted as if the creation, organization, and maintenance of church groups were human rights as intrinsic as the formation and direction of political institutions. In the Old World the church had been considered something given by God and regulated by his properly consecrated ministers. Except for a small dissenting fringe, European Christians into the nineteenth century did not entertain the idea that they were capable of creating churches and charting their courses. In America a different cast of mind prevailed; it was assumed that Christians had not only the right but also the duty to create ecclesiastical institutions as their own consciences demanded. This assumption produced both healthy and unhealthy effects: while it released the energy of countless creative individuals for the widest possible variety of Christian expressions, it also tended to make the churches unduly subject to the whims of their creators. The stability and continuity, if also stagnation, which had attended the Old World idea of *the* church gave way to the energetic competitiveness, if also eccentricity, of the church*es* in the New World. The peculiar shape of denominational life in America owed much to the ideology of freedom championed so successfully in the Revolutionary period.

The ideas of the Revolution touched American theology no less than ecclesiology. The crass identification of Patriotism and Christianity was later extrapolated into the facile identification of America as a Christian country and United States citizens as Christians by cultural birthright. This identification, however, has not affected theological life in America as much as a subtler and more pervasive phenomenon — the basic shift away from a Calvinistic orientation in theology. Where the identification of all American citizens as Christian believers falls apart upon even superficial analysis, the movement away from Calvinism presents a more complicated picture. The influence of libertarian thought on American theology has been noted by historians of the United States, but the extent of its impact, as well as the exact role of the Revolution in exerting that influence, deserves closer attention.

A convenient way of describing the general shift in American theology over the last half of the eighteenth and the first half of the nineteenth centuries is to examine the fate of the standard "five points" of Calvinism when confronted with the principles of the American Revolution. The first of the Calvinistic points, "total depravity," did not stand up well to the belief that individuals were inherently capable of shaping their own destinies. The earlier Puritans taught that human sinfulness prevented the unconverted person from performing any truly good deeds, including the act of turning from sin to God. Christians in the youthful United States continued to talk about the evil effects of sin, but they did not think that human evil deprived men of the power to determine their own religious or political destinies.

The concept of "unconditional election" also seemed to deny that men were fully capable of determining the course of their own lives. In the dominant colonial churches, the Calvinist teaching of election had maintained that it was God alone who, by an act of his sovereign will, called certain individuals to salvation. But if the establishment of a relationship with God was God's doing and not an individual's, it made a mockery of the conviction that each man had the inalienable right to secure happiness as a result of his own efforts.

The anti-democratic tendency of the doctrine of election emerged even more clearly in the idea of a "limited atonement." The Calvinist believed that the efficacy of Christ's death and resurrection was restricted to those whom God elected to salvation. But since Americans believed that all men were created equal in political matters, it was difficult to believe that God would arbitrarily limit the effects of the work of Christ to only a few. The egalitarian strain emerging from the Revolution could make no sense of such a wanton infringement upon natural rights.

Further, the concept of "irresistible grace" seemed inimical to the Whig conviction that uncontrollable power was evil. To say, as the Edwardsean Calvinists did, that people became Christians apart from the self-determined choice of their own wills seemed dangerously close to asserting that God exercised the kind of irresponsible power against which the colonies had rebelled.

The last of the Calvinistic principles, the "perseverance of the saints," was usually retained by American Christians, but for a new reason. A believer was sustained in the faith not as a result of God's power but because of the continuing effect of his own choice for God. The believer possessed the sure hope of eternal life as a due right in consequence of his own decision to become a Christian.

Individual believers and various denominations participated in this movement away from Calvinism in different degrees. Indeed, the Calvinistic orientation persisted for a considerable time among some of the groups, such as the Presbyterians, who most ardently supported Whig thought. On the other hand, the denominations which grew most rapidly in the post-Revolutionary period, Baptists and Methodists, expressed their theology to a greater or lesser degree in the new forms. The influence of Whig ideology was certainly not the only impetus hastening the decline of Calvinism in America, but it played one of the most important roles in the process. The attention which the Revolution had called to the concept of freedom altered the definition of this idea that had prevailed in the largely Calvinistic colonies. Freedom in the Revolutionary generation came to mean primarily freedom *from* something — from tyranny, oppression, and the arbitrary exercise of power. Freedom in the earlier Calvinistic sense of the word had implied freedom *for* something — for fulfillment and hope, found only in being overmastered by God. The change was subtle, and it was obscured due to the fact that the single word "freedom" was used to express two related, but also contrasting, ideas. The crisis atmosphere of the Revolutionary period further obscured the two senses of "freedom" and greatly facilitated the process in the American churches by which the Whig idea of liberty came to replace the Calvinistic concept.

Just as it has been important to keep in mind the different Christian responses to the Revolution, so it is necessary to remember that these generalizations concerning the impact of the Revolution on later American religious history did not apply equally to all groups of Christians. In particular, minority groups outside of the English Puritan tradition were insulated from some of the ecclesiastical and theological changes brought about by Revolutionary thought. Groups such as the Lutherans or the Mennonites who retained the language and ecclesiastical practices of the Old World naturally tended to participate less actively in the trends and innovations characteristic of the American religious landscape. Even in the domain of religious minorities, however, the Revolutionary period witnessed patterns that have marked later American history.

The majority religious and cultural viewpoint — in the Revolutionary period, the mixture of libertarianism and Christianity — exerted weighty pressure on minority viewpoints to conform. While the Continental Congress and individual colonial legislatures did make provision for certain deviations from majority policy, the pacifists and Loyalists were still pressured culturally to conform to the Patriotic Whig position. Throughout American history a similar pressure, occasionally official but more often unofficial, has continued to encourage the assimilation of minority religious perspectives into the prevailing majority pattern. Only in recent years have historians made clear how intense were these pressures on Lutherans, Quakers, Dunkers, and other smaller religious groups to adopt the perspectives and practices of mainstream religious bodies. Partially as a result of this external pressure and partly as a product of the desires of those within the minority groups, denominations such as the Quakers and Moravians gradually relinquished some of the doctrinal and practical distinctions which set them apart from the Protestant bodies of Puritan heritage. The Revolutionary period was by no means the only epoch which saw this process at work, but it was one of particularly intense pressure to conform to the common American mold.

From the perspective of the minority groups themselves, it has taken supreme effort and many sacrifices to preserve distinctive traits that did not conform to the prevailing American patterns. Rather than compromise their loyalties to Great Britain, many Anglicans and a smattering of individuals from other denominations migrated to Canada or returned to England. Religious groups in later American history have also been forced into flight, either geographic or psychic, in order to preserve minority religious perspectives. For Mormons in mid-nineteenth-century America, escape to the barren West provided a means to preserve religious distinctives. For fundamentalists in the early twentieth century, withdrawal from the intellectual, scientific, and artistic mainstreams of American culture provided a psychic means to maintain deeply held beliefs. Little substantial similarity exists between pacifist Mennonites of rural Pennsylvania in the eighteenth century and either nineteenth-century Mormons or twentieth-century fundamentalists, but the formal similarity is striking: in each case withdrawal preserved the essentials of a religiosity unacceptable to the majority socio-religious point of view in the country. The behavior of religious minorities during the Revolution has served more as a model of escape for, rather than a direct influence upon, other hard-pressed religious groups in the course of American history.

No history of the United States can claim our attention if it does not discuss the profound impact of the Revolutionary period on the future course of events in America. The ideas and actions which gave birth to a new nation or which emerged during that birth process constructed the foundation upon which subsequent American history has been built. Later men and women of ideas and actions have added distinctive personal touches to the edifice of American history, new ideas and patterns of behavior have altered its appearance significantly, and yet the foundation retains its fundamental importance.

In like manner, the religious history of the United States will never be adequately understood apart from a knowledge of Christian thought and behavior at the time of the Revolution. During this period believers were called upon to examine the elements of their religious heritages, and they responded by recasting many of them into new forms. For many believers the Revolution united religious beliefs and political principles into unified convictions about the proper nature of life as Christians and as American citizens. For a lesser number the Revolution called forth demanding sacrifices when personal convictions went against the grain of the Christian-Whig majority. The peculiarly American blending of religious, social, political, and cultural perspectives did not begin from scratch during the Revolution, but the period did encourage an interweaving of these various aspects of life. Throughout America's later history the relative strength of religious ideas vis-à-vis other forces in American culture has varied greatly, but the bond linking religion to all the other interests of life in society has never been broken.

A Note on Sources

*Even before interest in America's bicentennial stim*ulated authors and publishers to write and release new studies on the Revolutionary period, the literature on this formative era was voluminous. The role of religion in the Revolution has not received the attention that has been directed to political, social, and military aspects of that event, but it has been studied in a number of different contexts. The works mentioned in this Note on Sources were helpful both in showing the various ways in which Christians responded to the Revolution and in describing the changes which the Revolution brought about in the churches. The items mentioned here do not constitute an exhaustive listing of material bearing on this subject, but they do include many of the most important recent studies of the topic.

Two works from the past decade stand out as key analyses of the role of religion in the American Revolution. Alan Heimert argues in *Religion and the American Mind From the Great Awakening to the Revolution* (Cambridge: Harvard University Press, 1966) that defenders of the colonial Great Awakening (namely, the theological conservatives in the colonies) spearheaded the drive for independence and social reform in America, while the opponents of the revival (the theological liberals) were reluctant in the fight not only against Britain but also against social inequality in America. Bernard Bailyn's "Religion and Revolution: Three Biographical Studies," *Perspectives in American History,* Vol. IV (1970), 83-169, rejects Heimert's conclusions and argues that although religion was important in the lives of individual Americans, it did not exercise a consistent influence on the politics of the period. However much they may disagree with each other, these two accounts provide the essential starting points for the analysis of this subject. The student who makes an effort to grasp the nature of the disagreement between Heimert and Bailyn will be rewarded with fresh insights into the problems faced by historians in reconstructing the role of religion in Revolutionary America.

A recent article by Nathan O. Hatch, "The Origins of Civil Millennialism in America: New England Clergymen, War with France, and the Revolution," *William and Mary Quarterly,* 3rd ser., XXXI (July, 1974), 407-430, presents a convincing account of the process by which Patriotism and Christianity of Puritan heritage came to be joined so intimately during the Revolution. In this article and his new book, *The Sacred Cause of Liberty: Republican Thought and the Millennium in Revolutionary New England* (New Haven: Yale University Press, 1977), Hatch has provided the finest treatment to date of the ideological bonds linking Whiggery and eighteenth-century American Christianity. Other general treatments of the role of religion in the Revolution have appeared sporadically throughout the twentieth century. Claude H. Van Tyne's pioneering essay, "Influences of the Clergy, and of Religious and Sectarian Forces, on the American Revolution," *American Historical Review,* XIX (October, 1913), 44-64, set the tone for much later research into this topic by showing how ministers and other religious leaders participated in the formation and propagation of the ideology which led to rebellion. Alice M. Baldwin's *New England Clergy and the American Revolution* (Durham, N.C.: Duke University Press, 1928) continues to be a valuable treatment of the response of religious New England to the war. If our understanding of Revolutionary thinking has advanced since Baldwin published her study in 1928, the care with which she drew together widely scattered accounts of ministerial participation in the conflict continues to place students of the period in her debt.

Some twenty years after the publication of her

book-length treatment of religion in Revolutionary New England, Baldwin published a very helpful article on the connections between religion and Patriotism in the southern colonies, "Sowers of Sedition: The Political Theories of Some of the New Light Presbyterian Clergy of Virginia and North Carolina," *William and Mary Quarterly,* 3rd ser., V (January, 1948), 52-76. Like her study on New England, this article blazed new trails. Attention paid to New England had so dominated the study of secular and religious aspects of the Revolutionary period that little had been written on the interaction of religious and political forces in other areas of the country. Thomas O'Brien Hanley has recently added to our understanding of Revolutionary religion outside of New England with his study, *The American Revolution and Religion: Maryland 1770-1800* (Washington, D.C.: The Catholic University of America Press, 1971).

A number of interpretative articles written during the last twenty years by recognized masters of early American history have done much to stimulate further research into the connection of religion and the Revolution. They include: Sidney E. Mead, "American Protestantism During the Revolutionary Epoch," *Church History,* XXII (December, 1953), 279-297 (reprinted in Mead's *Lively Experiment* [New York: Harper & Row, 1963]); Perry Miller, "From the Covenant to the Revival," in *The Shaping of American Religion, Vol. I,* eds. James Ward Smith and A. Leland Jamison (Princeton: Princeton University Press, 1961); Edmund S. Morgan, "The Puritan Ethic and the American Revolution," *William and Mary Quarterly,* 3rd ser., XXIV (January, 1967), 3-43; and William G. McLoughlin, "The Role of Religion in the Revolution: Liberty of Conscience and Cultural Cohesion in the New Nation," in *Essays on the American Revolution,* eds. Stephen G. Kurtz and James H. Hutson (Chapel Hill, N.C.: University of North Carolina Press, 1973). Dagobert de Levie, a less well known author, has provided a helpful study of contrasting approaches to the Revolution in his article "Patriotic Activity of Calvinistic and Lutheran Clergymen during the American Revolution," *Lutheran Quarterly,* VIII (November, 1956), 319-340. More lengthy surveys of the general topic have been given by Cedric B. Cowing, *The Great Awakening and the American Revolution: Colonial Thought in the 18th Century* (Chicago: Rand McNally, 1971), and in the early chapters of Cushing Strout's *New Heavens and New Earth: Political Religion in America* (New York: Harper & Row, 1974).

Clifford K. Shipton has made available a uniquely valuable resource for the study of religion in Revolutionary America in his biographical portraits, *Sibley's Harvard Graduates* (vols. IV-XVII; Boston: Massachusetts Historical Society, 1933-1975). Shipton's subjects constitute a limited class in the colonies, but the scholarship, depth, and sensitivity of his sketches make them very useful tools in the study of the Patriots and Loyalists numbered among the graduates of Harvard College. Although Shipton was not writing ecclesiastical biographies, his treatment of the religious aspects of his subjects' lives is uniformly informative.

The titles of primary source materials that I have cited in the body of the text make up the barest fraction of the materials published during the Revolutionary period by clergymen on political subjects which used religion in the analysis of the political situation or discussed the effects of political decisions on the churches. The extensive notes in Alan Heimert's *Religion and the American Mind* provide a better indication of the scope of writing connecting religion and politics during the Revolution. Bibliographical information on the many works produced from 1750 to 1785 which dealt with religion and politics can be found in Charles Evans' *American Bibliography* (vols. I-XII; Chicago: privately printed for the author, 1903-1934; vols. XII-XIV; Worcester, Mass.: American Antiquarian Society, 1955-1959). Only by extensive reading in these original sources can one grasp the nature of religion's role in the Revolution. The works listed in Evans' *American Bibliography* are conveniently available in most major libraries through the Microcard edition of Early American Imprints edited by Clifford K. Shipton and produced by the American Antiquarian Society. Helpful introductions to this primary source material have been provided by John Wingate Thornton, ed., *The Pulpit of the*

*American Revolution: or, the Political Sermons of the Period
of 1776* (Boston: Gould & Lincoln, 1860), and Peter N.
Carroll, ed., *Religion and the Coming of the American Revolution* (Waltham, Mass.: Ginn-Blaisdell, 1970).

    While writing Chapter One I used many of the
standard accounts of the Revolutionary period. Useful documentary collections of the most important records covering
this period have been compiled by Henry Steele Commager,
ed., *Documents of American History, Volume I: To 1898*,
8th ed. (New York: Appleton-Century-Crofts, 1968), and
Samuel Eliot Morison, ed., *Sources & Documents illustrating
the American Revolution 1764-1788 and the formation of
the Federal Constitution*, 2nd ed. (New York: Oxford University Press, 1929 [paperback reprint, 1972]). Edmund S.
Morgan and Jack P. Greene have published valuable introductions to the various ways in which the significance of
the Revolution has been interpreted: Edmund S. Morgan,
ed., *The American Revolution: Two Centuries of Interpretation* (Englewood Cliffs, N.J.: Prentice-Hall, 1965); Jack
P. Greene, *The Reappraisal of the American Revolution in
Recent Historical Literature* (Washington, D.C.: American
Historical Association, 1967). These studies are of particular importance in delineating what different individuals
throughout American history have meant when speaking of
the American Revolution. Materials on the Revolutionary
period continue to proliferate, but the Library of Congress
has two fairly recent publications providing guidelines to
some of the most important literature on this subject: *The
American Revolution: A Selected Reading List* (1968);
*Periodical Literature on the American Revolution: Historical
Research and Changing Interpretations, 1895-1970*, compiled
by Ronald M. Gephart (1971). A more comprehensive bibliography is provided by John Shy in *The American Revolution*
(Northbrook, Ill.: AHM, 1973).

    I have followed Bernard Bailyn's *Ideological Ori-
gins of the American Revolution* (Cambridge: Belknap Press
of the Harvard University Press, 1967) in my description of
the thinking underlying the revolt. This lucid, solidly docu-
mented work is an indispensable guide to the ideas which

led to independence. The British background of the Whig thought which came to ascendancy in America has been described with insight by Caroline Robbins in *The Eighteenth-Century Commonwealthman: Studies in the Transmission, Development and Circumstance of English Liberal Thought from the Restoration of Charles II Until the War with the Thirteen Colonies* (Cambridge: Harvard University Press, 1959). Robert E. Shalhope provides a comprehensive overview of the currently most popular interpretation of the ideological background of the Revolution in his article "Toward a Republican Synthesis: The Emergence of an Understanding of Republicanism in American Historiography," *William and Mary Quarterly,* 3rd ser., XXIX (January, 1972), 49-80.

        Of the countless other books on the American Revolution which could be mentioned, J. Franklin Jameson's *American Revolution Considered as a Social Movement* (Princeton: Princeton University Press, 1926 [many paperback reprints]) deserves special mention. Although many of Jameson's specific conclusions concerning the social impact of the Revolution have been questioned since his study was published, the methodological assumption upon which the book is based continues to exert a constructive influence: "All the varied activities of men in the same country and period have had intimate relations with each other, and . . . one cannot obtain a satisfactory view of any one of them by considering it apart from the others." Jameson's example has encouraged historians to look at the Revolutionary period as a whole and not to rest content until the interrelationships between various aspects of life in Revolutionary America were perceived and understood. Jameson's conviction that the study of any given period must include these interrelationships has been an important foundation of my study.

        The early chapters of Sydney E. Ahlstrom's *Religious History of the American People* (New Haven: Yale University Press, 1972) and Winthrop S. Hudson's *Religion in America,* 2nd ed. (New York: Charles Scribner's Sons, 1973) provide well-written and reliable summaries of the general religious history of the colonial period. In addition to these narrative accounts, more particular studies of the Great Awakening and of its most prominent figures that were useful in the writing of Chapter Two include: Edwin Scott Gaustad, *The Great Awakening in New England* (New York: Harper & Brothers, 1957); Charles Hartshorn Maxson, *The Great Awakening in the Middle Colonies* (Chicago: University of Chicago Press, 1920 [reprinted Gloucester, Mass.: Peter Smith, 1958]); Wesley M. Gewehr, *The Great Awakening in Virginia, 1740-1790* (Durham, N.C.: Duke University Press, 1930 [reprinted Gloucester, Mass.: Peter Smith, 1965]); Perry Miller, *Jonathan Edwards* (New York: W. Sloane Associates, 1949); Ola Elizabeth Winslow, *Jonathan Edwards, 1703-1758* (New York: Macmillan, 1950); the critical introductions in the current Yale edition of Edwards' works; Stuart C. Henry, *George Whitefield: Wayfaring Witness* (Nashville: Abingdon, 1957); and Arnold Dallimore, *George Whitefield, Vol. I* (London: Banner of Truth, 1970).

Challenging new interpretations of the connection between the Great Awakening and the Revolution which came to my attention too late to be used for this volume are offered by Harry Stout in "The Great Awakening in New England Reconsidered: The New England Clergy," *Journal of Social History,* VIII (Fall 1974), 21-47; and "Religion, Communications and the Ideological Origins of the American Revolution," *Willam and Mary Quarterly* (forthcoming). Mention should be made as well of the valuable new survey, J. M. Bumsted and John E. Van de Wetering, *What must I do to be Saved? The Great Awakening in Colonial America* (Hinsdale, Illinois: Dryden, 1976).

The many works of Perry Miller on seventeenth- and eighteenth-century New England are still the places to begin study of the intellectual life of Puritanism in America. Of particular value for this study was his *New England Mind: From Colony to Province* (Cambridge: Harvard University Press, 1953). Miller's conclusions concerning New England have not gone unchallenged, and in his article "American Puritan Studies in the 1960s," *William and Mary Quarterly,* 3rd ser., XXVII (January, 1970), 36-37, Michael McGiffert provides a helpful summary of the most promising lines of Puritan studies since Miller.

There are not a great number of studies on the theology of eighteenth-century America. Three works which do attempt to describe the development of American religious thought in this period are Joseph Haroutunian, *Piety Versus Moralism: The Passing of the New England Theology* (New York: Henry Holt, 1932 [reprinted New York: Harper Torchbook, 1970]); Frank H. Foster, *A Genetic History of the New England Theology* (Chicago: University of Chicago Press, 1907); and Peter Y. DeJong, *The Covenant Idea in New England Theology, 1620-1847* (Grand Rapids: Eerdmans, 1945). Haroutunian's volume is a particularly insightful account of the shifts within New England religion at the time of the Revolution and immediately thereafter. Religious influences in the lives of the major Revolutionary figures are covered in their standard biographies. The Christian sensibilities of Samuel Adams and Patrick Henry, who were signaled out for special mention in the text, have been examined by William Appleman Williams, "Samuel Adams: Calvinist, Mercantilist, Revolutionary," *Studies on the Left,* Vol. I (Winter, 1960), 47-57; and George F. Willison, *Patrick Henry and His World* (Garden City, N.Y.: Doubleday, 1969), pp. 67-68, and 383.

The chapter on the Patriotic response to the Revolution is heavily indebted to the general studies of religion and the Revolution already mentioned. In addition, Nathan O. Hatch's 1974 dissertation from Washington University in St. Louis, on which his *Sacred Cause of Liberty* is based, offered a comprehensive framework and specific examples which were extremely helpful. The largely Patriotic response of the Presbyterians has received several solid and stimulating treatments: Leonard J. Trinterud, *The Forming of an American Tradition: A Re-examination of Colonial Presbyterianism* (Philadelphia: Westminster, 1949); Leonard J. Kramer, "Presbyterians Approach the American Revolution," *Journal of the Presbyterian Historical Society,* XXXI (June and September, 1953), 71-86 and 167-180, and "Muskets in the Pulpit, 1776-1783," *ibid.,* XXXI and XXXII (December,

1953, and March, 1954), 229-244 and 37-51; and James H. Smylie, "Presbyterian Clergy and Problems of 'Dominion' in the Revolutionary Generation," *Journal of Presbyterian History,* XLVIII (Fall, 1970), 161-175. These accounts and James L. McAllister's essay, "John Witherspoon: Academic Advocate for American Freedom," in *A Miscellany of American Christianity,* ed. Stuart C. Henry (Durham, N.C.: Duke University Press, 1963), helped greatly in my interpretation of John Witherspoon's Revolutionary activities. The *Journal of Presbyterian History* devoted its entire Winter, 1974, issue to a most interesting documentary account of Presbyterian involvement in the conflict. Material on Moses Mather is drawn from my dissertation, "Church Membership and the American Revolution: An Aspect of Religion and Society in New England from the Revival to the War for Independence" (unpublished Ph.D. dissertation, Vanderbilt University, 1975). Of the many valuable studies concerning the influence of religion on local conditions prior to the war, three on Connecticut are especially perceptive: Oscar Zeichner, *Connecticut's Years of Controversy, 1750-1776* (Chapel Hill, N.C.: University of North Carolina Press, 1949); Richard L. Bushman, *From Puritan to Yankee: Character and the Social Order in Connecticut, 1690-1765* (Cambridge: Harvard University Press, 1967); and Robert Sklar, "The Great Awakening and Colonial Politics: Connecticut's Revolution in the Minds of Men," *Connecticut Historical Society Bulletin,* XXVIII (July, 1963), 81-95.

Carl Bridenbaugh's *Mitre and Sceptre: Transatlantic Faiths, Ideas, Personalities, and Politics, 1689-1775* (New York: Oxford University Press, 1962) describes the origins, nature, and development of the colonists' fear of the Church of England. He argues convincingly that this fear was one of the principal factors in the estrangement of Great Britain and her colonies. Two excellent recent biographies make singular contributions to the study of religion and society in pre-Revolutionary and Revolutionary America: Edmund S. Morgan, *The Gentle Puritan: A Life of Ezra Stiles, 1727-1795* (New Haven: Yale University Press, 1962) and Charles W. Akers, *Called unto Liberty: A Life of Jonathan*

Mayhew, 1720-1766 (Cambridge: Harvard University Press, 1964). The pulpit rhetoric which fueled the drive for independence has been described in Harry P. Kerr's "Politics and Religion in Colonial Fast and Thanksgiving Sermons, 1763-1783," *The Quarterly Journal of Speech,* XLVI (December, 1960), 372-382; Kerr, "The Election Sermon: Primer for Revolutionaries," *Speech Monographs,* XXIX (March, 1962), 13-22; and Harold D. Mixon, "Boston's Artillery Election Sermons and the American Revolution," *Speech Monographs,* XXXIV (March, 1967), 43-50.

What I have called the reforming response to the Revolution has not received the treatment which the Patriotic position has been accorded. In *Ideological Origins of the American Revolution,* Bernard Bailyn touches on the religious component in what he calls "The Contagion of Liberty," that process by which the ideas embedded in the argument against Great Britain came to be applied to life in America. William G. McLoughlin's biography of Isaac Backus, *Isaac Backus and the American Pietistic Tradition* (Boston: Little, Brown, 1967), and his magisterial study, *New England Dissent 1630-1833: The Baptists and the Separation of Church and State,* 2 vols. (Cambridge: Harvard University Press, 1971), illuminate the nature of the Baptists' response to the Revolution. An excellent article by David S. Lovejoy, "Samuel Hopkins: Religion, Slavery, and the Revolution," *New England Quarterly,* XL (June, 1967), 227-243, traces Hopkins' anti-slavery sentiment to his religious convictions rather than to the influence of Real Whiggery. A valuable supplement to Lovejoy's treatment of Hopkins has been offered by David E. Swift, "Samuel Hopkins: Calvinist Social Concern in Eighteenth Century New England," *Journal of Presbyterian History,* XLVII (March, 1969), 31-54. Connections between the reforming response and contemporary theological and ecclesiological thought are explored in my dissertation, "Church Membership and the American Revolution."

General studies of Loyalism in Revolutionary America have come into their own in comparatively recent times. For a long while Lorenzo Sabine's *Biographical Sketches of Loyalists of the American Revolution, with An Historical*

Essay, 2 vols. (Boston: Little, Brown, 1864), dominated this important field of Revolutionary studies. Recent works such as William H. Nelson's *The American Tory* (Oxford: Clarendon Press, 1961), Catherine S. Crary's *The Price of Loyalty: Tory Writings from the Revolutionary Era* (New York: McGraw-Hill, 1973), and Robert McCluer Calhoon's *The Loyalists in Revolutionary America, 1760-1781* (New York: Harcourt Brace Jovanovich, 1973), have provided fresh and perceptive treatment of the colonial Loyalists. General histories of the Protestant Episcopal Church in America are of much help in reconstructing the reaction of Anglican Loyalists to the Revolution. Back issues of *The Historical Magazine of the Protestant Episcopal Church* constitute an invaluable treasure of particular studies concerning the thoughts and actions of American Anglicans during the Revolution. The religious perceptions lying behind the Loyalism of some Methodists, Roman Catholics, and Presbyterians are treated, respectively, by Lynwood M. Holland, "John Wesley and the American Revolution," *A Journal of Church and State,* V (November, 1963), 199-213, and Donald Baker, "Charles Wesley and the American War for Independence," *Methodist History,* V (October, 1966), 5-37; Charles H. Metzger, *Catholics and the American Revolution* (Chicago: Loyola University Press, 1962); and Robert O. DeMond, *The Loyalists in North Carolina during the Revolution* (Durham, N.C.: Duke University Press, 1940 [reprinted Hamden, Conn.: Archon Books, 1964]), and Marjorie Daniel, "John Joachim Zubly — Georgia Pamphleteer of the Revolution," *Georgia Historical Quarterly,* XIX (March, 1935), 1-16.

Peter Brock's massive *Pacifism in the United States: From the Colonial Era to the First World War* (Princeton: Princeton University Press, 1968) offers comprehensive coverage of pacifists during the American Revolution. Combining a broad grasp of primary source materials with perceptive interpretations, Brock's detailed study constitutes the definitive treatment of the peace churches in eighteenth-century America. Denominational publications such as the *Mennonite Quarterly Review* or the *Transactions of the Moravian Historical Society* are also very valuable resources for the study of pacifism in the Revolution. A recent issue of the *Men-nonite Historical Bulletin* (July, 1974) was, for example, given over to documentary records concerning actions taken by Mennonites at the start of the conflict. Journals from states in which the pacifist groups were concentrated during the Revolutionary period, such as the *North Carolina Historical Review* and the *Pennsylvania Magazine of History and Biography,* also contain informative articles on this aspect of religion in the Revolution. Denominational histories and biographical studies of major figures in the colonial histories of these bodies, such as Kenneth Gardiner Hamilton's *John Ettwein and the Moravian Church during the Revolutionary Period* (Bethlehem, Pa.: Times Publishing Co., 1940), also provide much detailed material that would otherwise be difficult to locate. A conference on "The Pacifist Conscience in a Revolutionary Age," held April 26, 1974, at Wesley Theological Seminary in Washington, D.C., and sponsored by The National Capital Area Bicentennial Consortium for Local History, greatly aided my thinking on the pacifist response to the Revolution. The pacifist leanings of Henry Melchior Muhlenberg have been detailed by Theodore G. Tappert in his article, "Henry Melchior Muhlenberg and the American Revolution," *Church History,* XI (September, 1942), 284-301. Ellen Star Brinton's article on "The Rogerenes," *New England Quarterly,* XVI (March, 1943), 3-19, includes some comment on their pacifist stance during the Revolution.

The influence of the Revolutionary period on the later religious history of America is an explicit or implicit theme of many studies treating the religious or intellectual life of nineteenth-century America. Edmund S. Morgan, "The American Revolution Considered as an Intellectual Movement," in *Paths of American Thought,* eds. Arthur M. Schlesinger, Jr., and Morton White (Boston: Houghton Mifflin, 1963), and James W. Davidson, "Searching for the Millennium: Problems for the 1790's and the 1970's," *New England Quarterly,* XLV (June, 1972), 241-261, deal specifically with the influence of the Revolutionary period on the fate of religion in the Federalist era. William Gribbin's treatment of religion during the War of 1812, *The Churches*

Militant (New Haven: Yale University Press, 1973), has obvious connections with the study of religion in the earlier war with Great Britain. H. Richard Niebuhr and Sacvan Bercovitch have included provocative material on the impact of the Revolutionary period in their general studies of the interrelationship of religion and society in the United States: H. Richard Niebuhr, "The Idea of the Covenant and American Democracy," *Church History,* XXIII (June, 1954), 126-135; Sacvan Bercovitch, "Horologicals to Chronometricals: The Rhetoric of the Jeremiad," in *Literary Monographs Volume 3,* ed. Eric Rothstein (Madison: University of Wisconsin Press, 1970), 1-124. A number of recent works have discussed the religious component in nineteenth-century conceptions of America's nature and destiny. In different ways these studies reinforce the conviction that patterns of religious and social interpenetration manifested during the Revolution developed into the prevailing socio-religious perceptions of the American people during the nineteenth century: Jerald C. Brauer, "The Rule of the Saints in American Politics," *Church History,* XXVII (September, 1958), 240-258; James Fulton Maclear, " 'The True American Union' of Church and State: The Reconstruction of the Theocratic Tradition," *Church History,* XXVIII (March, 1959), 41-62; Ernest Lee Tuveson, *Redeemer Nation: The Idea of America's Millennial Role* (Chicago: University of Chicago Press, 1968); Maclear, "The Republic and the Millennium," in *The Religion of the Republic,* ed. Elwyn A. Smith (Philadelphia: Fortress, 1971); Conrad Cherry, ed., *God's New Israel: Religious Interpretations of American Destiny* (Englewood Cliffs, N.J.: Prentice-Hall, 1971); and Paul C. Nagel, *This Sacred Trust: American Nationality 1798-1898* (New York: Oxford University Press, 1971).

The bicentennial year saw the publication of many valuable studies on religious aspects of the American Revolution. The ones I have read thus far do not alter my basic impressions of the period, but their contributions help sharpen the general picture drawn in this volume. Particular mention should be made of the journals which devoted entire issues to the theme of religion and the Revolution. Of those that

I have seen, the April-June 1976 issue of *Foundations,* the Spring 1976 issue of the *Journal of Presbyterian History,* and the September 1976 issue of *Church History* are especially helpful.

Those who have not had enough of my point of view may consult the following articles which expand upon certain aspects of this narrative and present, with less restraint, my opinions on the historical developments of the period: "The Church and the American Revolution: Historiographical Pitfalls, Problems, and Progress," *Fides et Historia,* VII (Fall 1975), 2-19; "Observations on the Reconciliation of Politics and Religion in Revolutionary New Jersey: The Case of Jacob Green," *Journal of Presbyterian History,* LIV (Summer 1976), 217-237; "Ebenezer Devotion: Religion and Society in Revolutionary Connecticut," *Church History,* XLV (September 1976), 293-307; and "Christian and Humanistic Values in Eighteenth-Century America: a Bicentennial Review," *Christian Scholar's Review,* VI (Nos. 2-3, 1976), 114-126.

Index